THE ESSENTIAL GUIDE TO
DRESSING

I am a dedicated advocate of the link between mindfulness and great personal style, and Jules Standish's new book, *The Essential Guide to Mindful Dressing*, excites in easy to follow steps that take you through the transformational process of learning to work beautifully with colour. Jules truly is 'the Queen of colour' in my opinion, passionate in the belief that we all have the potential to look incredible through colour. So if you do one thing just for 'you' this year, invest in Jules' book, as you buy into how lovely you can look and feel with her expert guidance to hand.
Wendy Elsmore, Director, *London College of Style*

In this hectic world when we cram so much into each day, gifted and insightful colour consultant Jules Standish gives you the benefit of her considerable knowledge and guides you through many situations giving you top tips all the way as to what colours, styles and make-up suit you using the clothes you already have in your wardrobe. Just adding a colourful scarf or jacket can make all the difference depending on your skin tone.

Mindful Dressing is sensitively and cleverly written being easy to understand and a book you will want to refer to time and again dealing with everyday situations giving ideas as to how colours can help. Situations might include: how to project yourself best for a job interview; how to look slimmer; through to more emotional circumstances such as coping with a bereavement or a divorce, or preparing yourself for your children to leave home.

Feel empowered by colourful mindful dressing. Go on experiment a little... You might just surprise yourself!
Jenny Cropper, *Action Medical Research Charity*

Every time Jules is on my show, she gives great advice about choosing the right colours to wear to feel fabulous. Her knowledge about the subject is amazing, having a positive impact on many people's lives who aren't happy with their image. Everyone needs to know the impact of colour and Jules is the right person to tell them!

Chrissy B, Producer and Presenter, *Chrissy B Show*

Jules' skills fully weave the science, physiological and neuro-logical with the everyday impact that colours have on us. She uses excellent well known examples like how Tiffany blue makes you feel fun loving and Nike red dynamic and exciting. This book is a valuable tool for both men and women to embrace colour by using Jules' experienced advice and guidance to take control of the image they project to the world and how people perceive them. It was inspiring to read the touching real life examples from people who have turned their life around by making clever colour choices, and Jules herself opens up about her own life particularly the empty nest syndrome and friends turning 50.

Kuldeep Channa, TV Producer and Director, Reiki Practitioner

I was fascinated, when Jules sent me her book, to find that her recommendations coincided precisely with my own experience. What is more, she has explored in depth the psychological reasons why people so frequently wear the 'wrong' colours, and I am sure that I shall for the rest of my days continue to find invaluable her advice on making oneself feel a great deal better through more appropriate colour choices. Nor does she leave it there: she explains in detail *how* to make these choices, and makes it all sound considerably less difficult than I might have imagined. A most welcome addition to the bookshelf of anyone (of either gender) who would like to feel younger, more confident or, quite simply, happier!

Ann Merivale, Deep Memory Process Therapist and Author of seven books, which include *Thicker Than Blood?*

The great novelist Anthony Trollope wrote, "My belief is that in life people will take you very much at your own reckoning." Having lived and worked on three continents I know that statement to be as true now as it was in the 1800s. That being the case, why would you not read and absorb the lessons from Jules Standish's excellent book? I have and they work; whether consciously or not we spend our lives choosing colours. Follow Jules' advice, think about your colours carefully and get them right. If you do it will change the way you feel.

It does not matter what sort of career you pursue or life you lead, but as Trollope said the way you feel about yourself is fundamental to the way your life will work out. As Jules writes, "Chasing an image that belongs to somebody else is rarely self-empowering." And if you do pursue a career in business remember that sage advice often attributed to a Mafia Don: "You never get a second chance to make a good first impression." How could anyone argue with that? Make that first impression count!
Andrew Sharpe, Company Director, Stockbroker

In *The Essential Guide to Mindful Dressing* Jules Standish has revealed original tips on colour as well as essential life skills. How fabulous to be in control of my life by choosing the right colour and shade to wear for maximum impact. I am an autumn and Jules has confirmed how to get the best out of my wardrobe whether in my studio working or at leisure with family and friends. I love her modern comparison with Mindfulness. She also explains how the right colours will support my immune system looking after my Mind–Body connections just as my Pilates exercise programmes do on a daily basis. *The Essential Guide to Mindful Dressing* is so empowering. I hope you enjoy it as much as I have!
Carina Bayley, Body Control Pilates Instructor and Studio Owner

The Essential Guide to Mindful Dressing

Choose Your Colours – Control Your Life

The Essential Guide to Mindful Dressing

Choose Your Colours – Control Your Life

Jules Standish

BOOKS

Winchester, UK
Washington, USA

First published by O-Books, 2016
O-Books is an imprint of John Hunt Publishing Ltd., Laurel House, Station Approach,
Alresford, Hants, SO24 9JH, UK
office1@jhpbooks.net
www.johnhuntpublishing.com

For distributor details and how to order please visit the 'Ordering' section on our website.

Text copyright: Jules Standish 2016

ISBN: 978 1 78535 492 2
978 1 78535 493 9 (ebook)
Library of Congress Control Number: 2016939773

A CIP catalogue record for this book is available from the British Library.

Design: Stuart Davies

Printed and bound by CPI Group (UK) Ltd, Croydon, CR0 4YY, UK

We operate a distinctive and ethical publishing philosophy in all
areas of our business, from our global network of authors to
production and worldwide distribution.

CONTENTS

Introduction

Mindfulness is all the rage – and now it can sort out your wardrobe! Wouldn't it be wonderful if every day you could feel happy, calm and in control, simply by choosing the right colours to wear; what could be more fabulous than that? My book tells you how! It reveals the secrets of how colours can make you radiate with happiness and well-being and how to achieve calm in a frantic world. This is the essential guide to mindful dressing, full of practical tips and advice to enhance all areas of your life through your wardrobe.

Have you ever wondered why sometimes you feel calm and composed wearing a certain colour, and yet in others bold, confident and energised? Do you recognise that certain colours actually make you feel happy and confident, whilst others tired, drained and exhausted?

Research shows that colours can have a psychological effect on your emotions boosting self-esteem and general well-being. You absorb colour through your eyes and your skin, so when you wear certain colours they trigger neurological responses in the brain which cause the hypothalamus gland to release feel good hormones. For instance it's no coincidence looking at a blue sea and sky makes you relaxed, and if you wear the colour blue it releases oxytocin, for stress busting and inducing a sense of calm. When you are happy and successful your brain releases dopamine giving you that warm, feel good buzz that we all crave and desperately need.

The skill of mindfulness is paying attention to your needs and taking control of your image so you can be more positive and productive. By focussing on and wearing your chosen colours you take your mind away from negative thoughts, anxieties, depression, stress and worry. Now you can choose to wear colours day and night that make you feel fabulous and it's all natural!

Being mindfully colourful not only projects a positive image but affects your health by boosting your immune system, aiding digestion, calming inflammation, increasing your metabolism and decreasing your blood pressure.

I put forward a new approach for you to discover how to choose your colours, the ones that will transform your life, and learn how to look and feel physically, psychologically and emotionally balanced and happy, today and every day.

Chapter 1

Mindful Matters... *and how to master your image*

It is not money that makes you well dressed: it is understanding.
Christian Dior

Wouldn't it be great if you could get into the habit of mindfully choosing your colours to suit your image every day? In order for this to happen, you firstly need to focus on your image and how you want to project yourself. Once you start to reap the benefits of looking and feeling your best, eventually with repetition you will mindfully choose colours with pleasure and ease.

Image is important as it defines who you are and expresses your personality giving you an identity. The word image literally means "the general impression that a person presents to the public". If your image was linked to a brand, what colour would you choose? Would you want to be recognised as UPS brown, reliable and dependable and someone who always delivers, or are you a Tiffany blue person, fun loving, imaginative and a great communicator? Perhaps you might want to be Nike red, someone who is exciting, dynamic and a real achiever? Companies spend a lot of time and money figuring out exactly what they want their brand to say about them, because the message they portray is vital to their business. Likewise, the colours that you choose to wear tell people about yourself.

The American writer Alison Lurie summarises the importance of image perfectly in her book *The Language of Clothes*, "For thousands of years human beings have communicated with one another first in the language of dress. Long before I am near enough to talk to you on the street, in a meeting, or at a party, you announce your sex, age and class to me through what you are wearing – and very possibly give me important information (or misinformation) as to your occupation, origin, personality, opinions, tastes, sexual desires and current mood."

If you mindfully begin each day by focussing on your image and what colours would help you emotionally and psychologically then you can choose to communicate your own personal message. Being aware of your colour choices will show results because your brain has a memory, and if you experience the enjoyment of a great day in a particular colour then you will feel positive and happy the next time you wear that colour, simply by an affirmative association.

So, you have the power to focus on choosing colours to enhance your image and the ones that make you smile. Also be mindful of the fact that your moods and body language are infectious to others around you: your family, friends, co-workers and random strangers on the bus!

It is possible to lose your image, or, perhaps you were never clear about it in the first place. You might have felt you were a more extroverted character in the past, someone who always loved to wear bright, warm shades of red and orange but as time and life have gone on have ended up in dark, muted and sombre colours. In this case, dark colours will be connected in some way to a difficult, melancholic period for you. Are you feeling the need to bring back some of that extroversion now? Over time and through difficult life experiences it is common to end up gravitating towards colours that really don't suit you or resonate with your personality or lifestyle anymore. Being mindfully aware of your needs, you will be able to choose the colours that suit you now.

I was involved in an interesting experiment that was carried out in *Psychologies Magazine*. They put an extroverted personality who normally wore bright colours in black for a week to see how she felt and how it affected her image. "I feel invisible walking down the street in black clothes" is how she summed up her experience as no one looked at her, or came up and chatted to her. She loved to look colourful and she was not happy with the results of changing her image – it didn't allow her personality to shine through and she felt dull and uninteresting.

The other woman in the experiment was a more introverted person and shied away from colour, choosing to live in black and white for a simple, classic look. However, when she was put into colours that she liked she felt "more playful, more like having fun". This wasn't trying to force her into anything too bright or uncomfortable, but simply introducing some soft, pastel shades that she felt complemented her personality and helped her feel more feminine, aside from the obvious benefit of making her face look years younger.

A wonderful example of someone who has embraced her image, however difficult, is Lizzie Velasquez. Lizzie has an undiagnosed syndrome which doesn't allow her to store fat or muscle, and as a result doesn't weigh more than 60 pounds, is tiny and looks years older than her actual age.

Whilst many women try to change themselves to fit in to the ideals of others' requirements, Lizzie seems to have learnt to accept herself with extraordinarily positive self-esteem. She is inspiring by her self-acceptance, and focussing on positive attributes of her image.

Throughout her childhood Lizzie prayed to be 'normal'. At school the other kids posted a video of her asking, "Is this the world's ugliest woman?" It got four million views and thousands of comments like: "Do the world a favour, put a gun to your head and kill yourself!"

She was devastated for a time but then slowly started to realise that her life was in her own hands and that she was not going to let her syndrome define her. She used their negativity to keep going and realised that by being grateful she could define herself by all the good things that she has; for instance, although blind in one eye she is thankful to be able to see through the other one.

Lizzie decided to turn her handicaps into something positive; she has written books and does talks all over the world, helping people to see that through her bravery and acceptance of who she is and how she looks she is proud of herself and pleased to be visible in front of all those people. Lizzie proved to herself that self-esteem is possible in all circumstances and, however badly you may feel about yourself, by focussing on the positive you can redefine who you are. It is wonderful to see her wearing such bright and confident colours, a true sign that she is now able to accept herself and finally enjoy her public persona.

Chasing an image that belongs to somebody else is rarely self-empowering. You can claim your own image through acceptance and choose colours mindfully that make you smile and feel confident and happy.

For many people real or imagined faults can mean not enjoying their bodies or clothes. I meet so many men and women who hate to shop because they feel lost among all the high fashions and not confident enough to know what suits them best as they get older. How many women (including yourself) in particular do you know who don't feel slim enough or have good enough features to accept and love themselves? How great to be able to embrace who you are and define your image which will in turn increase your confidence by acceptance. It is incredibly attractive to meet someone who is content in their own skin. As the journalist Amanda Platell commented, "Who could be attracted to a woman who clearly doesn't value herself enough to make the most of her appearance – to a woman who seems to want to disappear?"

Image is intrinsically linked to self-esteem. This is fundamentally different to self-confidence, which the dictionary defines as being "a strong belief in one's own ability to achieve", whereas self-esteem is "an awareness of the value of one's own character".

As Mia Törnblom writes in her book *Self-Esteem Now!*: "If your self-esteem is low, you never know what you're worth. It fluctuates according to who's around you at the time. It's impossible to regard yourself as an equal. You're either better, or worse. If you want love and respect, you have to begin by recognising your own importance. You are neither more nor less important that other people in social settings, but to yourself you are actually the most important thing in the whole world."

This of course is often no more acutely felt than in a working environment where it is easy to sometimes feel that somebody else is better than you are. You need to feel that you are worthy of your position and your status within your chosen career, and feeling good about yourself on the inside can be projected positively through your appearance and image.

In business first impressions are vital because ninety per cent of people will form an opinion within the first 10–40 seconds of meeting you. Also 93% of first impressions are taken on how you look and sound, and only 7% on what is actually said. The most important rule in projecting a positive, professional image is to be well dressed. This gives self-confidence which leads to improved work relationships and increased performance, otherwise known as "The Circle of Success".

Anika was in her early 40s when she came to me because she was struggling at work. She didn't feel confident about herself and as a result wasn't managing to bring in the business that was required. She wore black every day, and being Asian this meant that with her dark hair and skin she felt she was able to go about her business without making a statement or standing out so in fact she was really endorsing the message "I am invisible". As her meetings were not being turned into positive deals she wondered if her image was letting her down. What was particularly interesting about Anika was initially she told me she had no idea why she didn't like colours and there was absolutely no reason for her not to wear them at work.

However, just as she was leaving she turned to me and said

she wasn't looking forward to the weekend because she would have to dress in bright coloured saris as this was expected as part of her culture. Of course, immediately she said it, I knew this was the reason she wore so much black and had veered away from colours when given the freedom to choose. How fascinating to see that on a subconscious level she had been made to wear these bright colours against her will, so when she had a choice she automatically kept away from them and stuck with dark clothing that she hadn't been forced to wear. So much of our conditioning and upbringing influences our feelings about colours.

In Anika's case she was using black not just as a uniform for work but because, as we discovered, she had a real problem with wearing bright colours. Now that she had brought this issue to the forefront of her mind, she was able to focus on choosing certain shades of colours she was attracted to which happened to be blue and pink, so as an experiment I asked her to add one of these colours in a shirt with her black suits. I wanted to see how this changed the way she felt about herself, making a conscious choice to wear a colour that appealed to her, i.e. nothing bright like her saris.

As confidence in business is vital in projecting an image of knowledge and skill it was paramount that Anika felt good about how she looked and wasn't simply doing it to please me! After a month she reported back that having consciously chosen to wear pink she felt more feminine and in touch with her emotions. Much to her surprise not only did she enjoy putting some colour into her everyday wardrobe but she also started clinching more deals. In Anika's case, being mindful about choosing the right colours and shades that really made her feel in control and confident had changed her image and the way that she performed at work.

Another wonderful example of how being mindful of colours can have amazing and positive benefits to image and self-esteem involves a man called David who worked in a corporate environment and was very unsure of his image, and therefore had little interest in his attire. He wore drab washed-out shades of greys and white, and didn't realise what a disservice the lack of colour was doing not only to his looks, but to his job as he felt unnoticed.

I knew David would be a challenge; however, once I put him in front of a mirror and draped some strong shades of blue combined with brighter ones up against his face his whole complexion looked rosy and healthy, and his blue eyes stood out and sparkled to such an extent I watched him start to smile and his whole demeanour changed into pride at the positive change in the way he looked.

David went home and told his wife his entire wardrobe needed updating in brighter, bolder colours, and having then gone shopping he turned up to work the following week wearing all his new shades of blue. Apparently he got so many compliments that he began to mindfully choose his colours which changed not only the way he felt about himself but how others reacted to him in the workplace as well.

The truth is that when you feel good about yourself, this has a positive effect on your image and people believe that you are indeed self-assured and someone who means business. That endorsement can then lead on to greater achievements both personally and professionally.

What's important is that you can control how you portray yourself to the outside world, by choosing the colours that make you look and feel fabulous every day. So start at the most visible place which will get you immediate results – your image!

Why Colour Your Image?

Being mindful about your colours and changing your wardrobe doesn't have to mean wearing bright green from head to toe and imitating a lime! Nor does it mean ditching everything in your wardrobe and starting again. It means adding some colour into your outfits to start feeling happier and healthier, lifting your moods and your general well-being and looking your best.

So how can colour have a powerful and transformational effect on your image? The physical benefits of wearing the right colours on the skin can be wonderfully positive and it really is immediate. The moment you put a shade that harmonises with your skin tone up against your face you can change the appearance of your complexion and your features will simply come alive. It is possible to take years off your age and give yourself that 'wow you look well today' appearance that wearing great colours can do instantly.

Many people believe that as you age you should morph into darker more sombre colours, but the opposite can be true. Brighter colours are youthful and fun loving, uplifting and dynamic, whereas dark shades can be incredibly ageing and draining.

I had the experience of consulting a woman in her late 50s who was looking for a new relationship and wanted to look her best. She wore a lot of black and dark colours, and was finding herself becoming increasingly depressed because she knew her wardrobe wasn't making her feel her most attractive or happy.

When she discovered that in fact she should be wearing warm light shades she felt instantly better (smiling every time one of her new colours was put on her) and not only did her mood lift but within a week of wearing her new clothes she started dating again!

Whatever image you are trying to portray for any given moment, day or event, consider in a mindful way what colours would serve you best. For instance, what colour would best work for a job interview? Are you going to meet a friend or partner to discuss a difficult issue and need good communication skills? Or are you recovering from an illness or depression, or maybe you simply need to unwind after a tiring day with a good night's sleep? For any of these events you could choose a shade of blue that suits your skin tone and colouring. Blue will increase your oxytocin, the feel good hormone that helps you relax and feel calm.

What about wearing red, the colour that releases adrenaline and will give you an energy boost if you are lacking in energy? If red is one of your favourite colours then find out what shade suits you best and wear this 'hot' colour on a new date as research proves men love to see women in red.

Every colour has a purpose, an influence and a power to change the way you look and feel about yourself and the way others view you. Now you can choose to control your image and get complimented every day by discovering the colours that suit you best at any given time and make your life a happier and more fulfilled place.

Your image matters, so mindfully take control of your colours for ultimate well-being and looking fabulous.

Chapter 2

Ageing Is All In the Mind... *and how colours can change your outlook*

And the beauty of a woman with passing years only grows!
Audrey Hepburn

In this current time of youthful promotion, ageing has become a bad word, not one that my mother or grandmother would recognise. The middle years of our lives should be an exciting time of self-discovery and contentment. We can dress to please ourselves and can feel empowered by making our own choices, treating ourselves as we get older and not worrying about what others think. Age used to have traditional transitions but nowadays it's more about state of mind than a number.

Personally I feel that ageing well isn't just about looking attractive to others, it's about valuing yourself; if you look after yourself and have pride in your appearance because you believe you are worth it, then others will too.

Part of the problem is that our culture ignores and patronises the elderly. Just read any paper to find famous, clever, beautiful women in the public domain who have all either been fired, downgraded in their career or simply ignored the moment they turned 50. The gorgeous presenter Mariella Frostrup recently said, "I shed half my workload the moment 50 appeared on my CV. Over 50s are an affluent, active, culturally ravenous bunch."

Apparently in the past year, more than 34,000 people over 50 have started an apprenticeship, so the tide is finally turning. However, ageing shouldn't be defined by a number, but how you view yourself. The ageing process can sap you of confidence as it can be a time of massive upheaval and change, particularly for women as it often kicks in at the start of the menopause.

Hair suddenly developing the texture of dried grass, added weight that has snuck up from behind and assaulted bottoms and stomachs, along with the added nightmare of constant fanning in public to cool down, mean that sometimes it is really hard to feel attractive and keep smiling.

Both women and men can also find themselves struggling with and juggling many issues at a time when they are experiencing major emotional changes too: empty nest syndrome, divorce, downsizing homes, retiring or looking after elderly parents.

When I turned 50, my daughter left home and, almost to the day, the hot flushes started. Not only was I entering menopause but also coping with empty nest syndrome. It was a time of deep distress for me, because the grief I felt at having a silent house combined with the physical changes to my body were enough to make me want to eat constantly, start smoking again and wear onesies day and night!

So how did I cope? Being a colour consultant and stylist I knew how to make positive decisions on what to wear. By mindfully choosing my best colours (the ones that suit my skin tone, that make me happy and get complimented in) I felt good about myself. I also took a long, hard and objective look at my wardrobe and gave myself a strict clear-out, keeping only the favoured items that really suit my colouring, body shape and lifestyle. It was incredibly cathartic.

My conscious clothing choices have become even more vitally important to my self-esteem than at any other time in my life. I still want to be visible, just perhaps not in such an obvious way as I did 20 years ago and, whilst I certainly can't cope with the 'mutton' label, I don't want to look old and frumpy either! This is a dilemma I come across a lot with women when they start to age. For many of us looks play a pivotal role in feeling confident about ourselves, so naturally we become afraid of grey hairs, wrinkles and loose chins hence the panicked outpouring of finances on anti-ageing products and in some cases desperate cosmetic procedures.

For me, long gone are the black 'do not approach I'm too cool' outfits of my teens and 'I'm a disco queen' bright turquoise eye shadow and matching tops of my twenties. Looking good now in my 50s is about understanding what colours suit me, what shade to keep my hair, how to wear my make-up and this also means making the most of what I have – wobbly, wrinkly bits and all – and giving myself permission to be seen in a way that makes me feel happy and confident about myself.

I cannot stress enough how important it is to know and wear the colours that really suit you as you tackle your own ageing process. We all managed to get away with things that didn't quite work in younger decades, however, the difficult reality is that the ageing process highlights all our detrimental issues and there is nowhere to hide!

If you are experiencing your own ageing process, the key is to discover which colours make YOU look attractive and feel fabulous and get you complimented, and which ones make YOU look old, tired and washed out and should be avoided. Can you wear black well against your face or do you look younger in blue? If so what shade of blue suits you? Some blues will make you look youthful and healthy, with an even skin tone whilst highlighting your attractive features. Others, however, may age you dramatically, bringing out the dark shadows, wrinkles and frown lines.

Choosing to wear harmonising colours up against your face will bring out the best of your complexion because they are matching your underlying skin tone making the skin look even, youthful and healthy. Equally the wrong colours will do the opposite and can make you look older, in some cases by many years.

For women looking fabulous is also about the colour make-up you wear because it creates the face you put on to the world. Skin tone changes as you age, so discovering what your best colour cosmetics are will make you look healthy with an even complexion, your eyes will sparkle and your cheekbones will be accentuated. All your features will come alive and help you to look youthful and healthy, whilst the wrong colours can drain your complexion and highlight negative ageing issues.

Let's not forget about hair colour. It needs to harmonise with your skin tone and not fight against it. So many women whilst tackling the ageing process opt for the wrong shades when the first signs of grey appear, which can in fact be more ageing than leaving it natural. If you do choose to colour your hair then you must opt for shades that complement your natural colour pigmentation; this is vital if you want to ensure you look great.

For most women and men at any age, discovering their true colours is a revelation but particularly as you start to lose your own natural colouring it becomes more important to get it right. Once discovered, you can feel like a new, younger and happier person, and will instantly want to transport your colour palette into your wardrobe.

Colour can also be used positively to camouflage the dodgy bits of middle age (spread!) and ensure your best bits (and you will have some!) are made visible. Mindfully choosing and wearing your colours then also becomes a lifestyle choice. Thelma van der Werff in her book *Let Colour Be Thy Medicine* says, "Waking up in the morning and choosing a colour that sets the tone of our day and supports our goals, or counteracts a negative feeling we may be having can be a powerful tool when wielded with intention. We all live a life that's as dull or as vibrant as our colour choices. Imagine what life could be if we were to use *all* the colours in a balanced way."

Recently I gave a talk to a group of schoolteachers and my objective was to help inspire them to think mindfully about how to wear colours so that they looked authoritative, yet were also still reaching out to young children, who are wonderfully reactive to colour.

That day I mindfully chose my outfit for the event. What I needed were good communication skills to get my message across but in a professional manner. I chose to wear a grey skirt, a businesslike colour that signifies self-control, wisdom, and the ability to handle situations in a practical and calm way. Having got the neutral colour sorted out I then chose a turquoise jacket. This is a shade of blue that I particularly favour and one of the shades of blue that I get complimented in.

Turquoise portrays an imaginative and creative person, who is sensitive to the needs of others and, as blue is the colour of communication, diplomacy and trust, I hoped it would help engage my audience in a way they found interesting and educational. So my choices for this speech were totally conscious, and as a 50 year old professional woman I wanted to inspire others to look and feel fabulous in their jobs as well as in their private lives.

Understanding what colours to wear, what coloured make-up suits you best, be it natural or dramatic along with hair colour that harmonises with your skin tone, can instantly make you look years younger. I often have women telling me they feel like they have had a facelift when they start wearing colours that make them look and feel fabulous. Now you can too!

Most of us experience challenging emotional periods at some time in our lives, but there is no reason why you can't still feel energised, sexy and positive. Whilst extra weight might be sneaking up on your hips, or hot flushes turning you into a secret stripper, colours can be transformational in helping with issues you may be experiencing right now.

Menopause and Ageing

Personally I think women entering menopause should be given 'sense of humour' pills along with HRT! Coping physically and emotionally can be like a rollercoaster ride, and whilst some lucky women might not experience problems there are many, like me, who do.

The menopause is not an illness and should therefore not be seen as a negative period in a woman's life – something to fear and dread. It is a natural event and should be experienced as a positive transition into a different phase. Most women's views on menopause are directly linked to their socio-economic status. In parts of Asia, for instance, it is seen as a time of liberation: free from the anxiety of unwanted pregnancy and the start of an age of real wisdom. In the Western world it is seen more as a problem time, when we can lose our femininity and start to age dramatically.

Medically speaking Dr Marilyn Glenville, PhD, sums it up simply in her brilliant book *New Natural Alternatives to HRT*: "The menopause happens because you have literally run out of eggs. Strictly speaking, the menopause is your very last period."

However, these changes can also be put down to ageing. Marilyn Glenville says, "Many so-called 'menopausal symptoms' may have little to do with the menopause. Some are just a natural part of the ageing process – think of irritability, declining libido, weight gain, ageing skin and hair, depression and anxiety. Some symptoms may also be related to a particular life-stage rather than hormones."

I was giving a talk last year to a group of professional women and one of them put her hand up and asked me how to cope now that she had entered the menopause and her hair had gone white, and her skin pale. She said, "I look in the mirror and I don't recognise myself anymore, I feel invisible." There was silence in the audience whilst many women nodded in agreement. I spent the rest of the talk showing these women how to put colour back into their fading looks to help them understand they could all continue to feel and look great.

For those of you who are through the menopause there is no reason why in your 60s, 70s and beyond you shouldn't continue to look fabulous. Many women in this age group think that wearing dark colours "reflect" their age, and that bright ones are too "young". What a mistake! The temptation when your hair goes white or grey and cools down your complexion is to cool down your wardrobe too. The truth is that whilst your skin may have gone paler with age, wearing cool pastel or dark shades is not always what it needs to look its best.

Your skin tone is hereditary which means you are either born with a warm, yellow/golden based complexion (even if pale) or a pink, cool based one. As you go through your life, your skin will change, due to the seasons, tanning, illness and ageing. However, skin never loses its base, i.e. remains cool or warm right through till the end of your life. So even though your hair may go silvery grey, your complexion if warm will remain so. In this case the most detrimental and ageing thing you can do is to wear cool shades to offset your hair colour.

A beautifully elegant lady in her 70s came to have a colour consultation with me as her daughter was worried that all the cool pastel shades of lavender and blue that she was wearing were washing her out and making her look really unwell. What stood out to me when she walked in was how white her hair was because it was harmonising with her jumper, which was an icy blue. Her underlying warm skin tone had been lost under her cool hair and clothing, so that her white hair was the focal point. Her true colours were warm and vibrant, and the next time we met she looked amazing: her eyes shone, her skin glowed and finally her face had become the focus and not her hair. She felt years younger and looked really healthy and well – no longer a pale skin lost amongst white hair.

So, the truth is that most women want to keep looking and feeling as attractive as possible throughout the menopause and into old age. As both are completely natural phases of a woman's life why not treat them naturally? This is where colour can really help.

How Can Colour Help?

The ageing process is a time to re-evaluate your appearance as it's so often not realised that colour is important to your looks and your well-being until the colours have gone. Complexion and hair colour fade during ageing and the menopause so it is vitally important to understand how to inject colour back into your life to ensure you stay looking attractive, healthy and feeling full of self-esteem.

Colour has the power to make you look better because it can take years off your face by giving an instant facelift, with none of the pain or high costs. Colour also has the power to make you feel better because it is absorbed through your skin and eyes, and affects your hormones – lifting your spirits and emotions.

If you are one of the many women who have a tendency to hot flushes you will know how embarrassing it can be. Did you know that wearing pink make-up can actually make you look even more flushed? Using peach and coral tones will counteract the redness as will wearing green up against your face. It will become your favourite colour! It is the complementary (opposite on the colour wheel) to red/pink and it automatically tones down a flushed complexion (whether you are wearing make-up or not).

Warm and cool colours can be used in different ways depending on your needs which can change daily, so it is important to know what you require physically and emotionally, and to understand the properties of each colour and their power to help you. Colour is natural. The menopause and ageing is natural. Combine them for optimum well-being.

Top colour tips for help with menopause and ageing:

- Wear green to feel physically balanced and to counteract facial redness if you suffer from a high cheek colour and hot flushes.
- Choose blue if you need calming down during panic attacks or stress during the menopause and also wear at

night to help you sleep better.
- Red clothing will help increase your energy when feeling tired and lethargic.
- Pink is the colour of love and will make you feel more feminine.
- Orange is a great colour to wear if you are needing some confidence at social events.
- Peach make-up with a yellow base can help to alleviate a high pink cheek colour.

Going back to work or getting a new job

Getting back into the job market after many years at home can be hugely daunting and, for many women in particular, bringing up a family has left them feeling unconfident. The thought of being in an office surrounded by trendy young things and being 'the oldie' is enough to make anyone head to the surgeon's office for some nips and tucks!

Combine the panic about wrinkles and sagging bottoms with lack of computer knowledge that the kids today seem to have in abundance – having been brought up on Facebook and Smart Chat – and it's enough to make any ageing woman hide under a comfy duvet.

What's really important is if you have chosen to go back to work or are embarking on a new career, you need to decide how you are going to present yourself. The styles and colours you wear, your make-up and your hair will all play a massive part in whether you actually get employed or not.

The first impression you make to a future employer is vital. The most important part in projecting a positive, professional image is to be well dressed. Research has proved that applicants get rejected because of poor personal appearance. The first thing you have to sell is yourself!

The brilliant book *The New Professional Image* written by Susan Bixler and Nancy Nix-Rice tells us, "Attractive wardrobe choices harmonise with your personal colouring, flatter your body shape, and enhance your features. Some people mistakenly believe that attractiveness is somehow a 'lightweight' concern that is not relevant in business. But the truth is, attractive sells, whether attaining it requires little work or a great deal of time and attention."

As your image is the first thing a potential employer notices, think carefully about your colour choices in your dress code. You will have certain colours that make you look and feel your best. There are, however, generally colours that will be more appropriate for certain interviews and jobs than others. Working in a media based company means your attire can be more casual with a creative edge, whilst the financial fields will require you to be more conservative, communicating a message of competence. Similarly for a job in the caring professions, wearing a severe black outfit would not project an image of compassion that those around you will be able to relate to.

Basic dark neutrals in blues, greys and blacks for jackets, suits, skirts and trousers work with softer colours in shirts, tops, scarves and dresses. Bright shades are often inappropriate for most businesses except perhaps fashion, design and art companies. Brown is generally not a good business colour, and should be kept for 'country' wear, except for camel, beige and stone which are very useful and mix well with lots of shades.

Florals and patterns should be avoided for interviews unless going into a creative environment where you will have more scope to express your personality. Keep your outfit simple, effective and make sure that all of you is well groomed, to include your hair and make-up. This will ensure you not only get the job you want, but keep it too!

You can create the visibility you want for any job. Take control and be impressive!

Top colour tips for job interviews:

- Blue is THE best colour for an interview as it's the colour of communication and therefore wonderful to help you express yourself in a calm and relaxed manner. Navy is a no-nonsense colour that means business – combine with cream for a smart look.
- Mid/dark grey is smart and mixes well with softer shades of pink, blue and yellow.
- Black trousers or skirts are always smart.
- If you wear black as a jacket use a good colour in a shirt to ensure your complexion looks its most attractive and healthy. For maximum impact black looks most dynamic when worn with red.
- Camel, beige and stone are all good neutrals in the warmer months.
- Avoid bright neon colours for interviews.

Empty Nest Syndrome

Whilst men also suffer when their family diminishes, it seems a cruel twist of fate that so many women who go through the menopause and start ageing dramatically often have to go through the pain of their children leaving home at the same time. For me it felt like I had lost something very deep inside me. My role as a mother had suddenly changed because I was no longer needed in the same way. It left me feeling redundant and empty. I understood finally why my own mother had suffered so much when I happily waved goodbye to her at the airport aged 18 not realising that she would cry and cry for days.

I see many women in my studio that have suddenly entered this very unsettling period in their lives. When you have nurtured a family and devoted years of your life to bringing up children, it feels like your job has suddenly been terminated which leaves you re-evaluating the rest of your life.

In most cases women feel they have simply lost their way. If this applies to you then your body may also now be a different shape, you may feel your looks have started to fade and that you don't suit the same clothes or colours that you wore 20 years ago. This has then left you feeling very insecure and unconfident.

If your image has changed, there is potentially a need to recreate yourself in a way that works for your lifestyle. The aim is to learn how to dress appropriately without trying to be too young or too old, looking great for your age and gaining the confidence you deserve.

Colour plays a vital part in lifting moods and creating a feeling of well-being. Not only will the clothes you now wear make you feel more positively about this next phase of your life, but the colours you put on your face will brighten your complexion and make you look healthy and confident. Your hair colour also needs to harmonise with your skin tone so that you don't look older.

Top colour tips for coping with empty nest syndrome:

- Red for facing new challenges and going back to work or changing jobs.
- Yellow for detaching from old habits so you can move forward.
- Purple for self-respect.
- Gold or silver instead of black for evening wear to look younger and help you to shine.
- Green for balance and harmony in your life.

Grief and Depression

The loss of a loved one whether it is a relative, friend or pet can make you feel pain and sadness. It's not just losing a loved one that can cause grief, but a number of different traumatic situations, such as divorce, losing a job, retirement, the break-up of a relationship, financial loss or children leaving home.

The brilliant psychiatrist Elisabeth Kübler-Ross through her work devised the "five stages of grief", which included denial, anger, bargaining, depression and acceptance. However, she accepted not everyone experienced all of these stages as people are all individual.

There are no hard and fast rules for getting through grief, and I have seen many people who have had colour consultations to discover which colours would best support them whilst in the 'recovery' period.

During the grieving process it is quite normal to want to become entirely invisible. This can often mean disappearing into dark colours and, particularly, black. However, this grieving or mourning period can be absolutely necessary. The time for intro-version and privacy during a time of intense crisis is often the first way of learning how to cope. For this reason it is important not to force yourself out of any emotional situation until absolutely ready.

Women can also suffer from feeling invisible within their marriages. The grief that is felt at being unhappy, unloved or unnoticed can be reflected in the way you look and how you dress.

Judith was married for 45 years to a man who had a very dominant and overpowering personality. As a result she learnt to be very obliging, and became compliant and sometimes intro-verted. After all her sacrifices, he left her anyway. Judith was a very outgoing, fun loving woman when she first got married and wore bright reds, oranges and yellows; but over the years, as she became more and more worn down, her clothing became pale, pastel and washed out. She says, "I look back and realise I lost a sense of myself in order to keep the peace." She remained in these dull pale colours for the first few years after her divorce. When she felt ready to be more like her old self again, she came to learn what her true colours were. Of course, they were the bright colours of her youth which made her then feel able to embrace her real personality after all this time, because they made her feel alive and happy again.

There is a difference between grief and depression. Ase Greenacre, a counsellor and life coach says that, "The time it takes to move out of grief depends upon your personality and your background experiences from before the trauma, as well as the level of support surrounding you. Often depression comes into play if there are unresolved issues from the past that have not been dealt with and then the current trauma simply becomes overwhelming and you can't move on."

When you lose someone close it can have devastating conse-quences, whatever your age and circumstances. Elizabeth lost her beloved husband when she was in her early 50s and has had to bring up two children under the age of ten. Her grief was immense, and even though she had a really strong support network of friends and family around her, she felt like her world had simply fallen apart.

I made sure that every time I saw her I gave her something purple to help heal her, whether it was flowers, a scarf or a picture. Purple is the highest spiritual colour and has the ability to calm the pains of the mind and to restore peace out of chaos. It also signals great change, transformation and learning that can come from deep pain. This has helped her take a more spiritual and deeper look at the meaning of her life and her future path.

Top colour tips for dealing with grief or depression:

- Wear shades of purple to help feel emotionally stronger and more stable.
- Violet clothing can help to heal a broken heart.
- Orange's vitality can help to shift depression, so wear it or choose amber coloured jewellery or orange accessories.
- Pink creates a loving environment and helps to make you feel feminine.
- Yellow is a wonderful colour to wear if you want to put some joy back into your life.

- Wear red if you are going out on a new date or want to inject some romance into an established relationship.

Illness

Not feeling well often means not having much energy or desire to make yourself look good, and can make you want to disappear and hibernate until recovery, whether it's the flu or a more serious illness. You will know how even the common cold can make you look peaky, with a red nose and blotchy skin. If you have experienced an illness that continued over long periods of time you may feel that not only your looks have suffered but your self-esteem too.

I had the pleasure of meeting a lovely woman who, in her 50s, had been through breast cancer and, having had treatment and gone into remission, was keen to know what colours she should wear to bring some well needed colour back into her appearance. The chemotherapy meant that her hair had fallen out and grown back almost white, her skin had taken on a grey pallor with a puffiness that had yet to dissipate. Her colouring had all but vanished, and she felt totally invisible.

Putting some feminine shades of pink, purple and turquoise blue up against her face made her smile with joy. She suddenly looked so much healthier and it had been a long time since she had been able to feel happy looking at herself in the mirror.

We discussed what hair colour would now harmonise with her skin tone and what colour make-up would give her complexion the glow she needed. She contacted me a few weeks after the consultation to tell me that, not only did she feel great because she loved all the colours, but people were commenting on how she looked "better than before she got ill". Colour had helped her recover emotionally and physically, and enabled her to look forward to a future looking better than ever.

The model Naomi Campbell's mother Valerie Morris came through breast cancer treatment and she publicly summed up how she felt afterwards, "Now I see and appreciate the detail in life, as if someone's turned up the colour. I've found myself again and I want other women going through it to know that's possible." Indeed, you can find yourself too, so turn up the colour in your life to help you recover. Just choose the one(s) that make you feel really happy and joyous and wear them in abundance!

Top colour tips for getting over an illness:

- Wearing green helps to cool the blood and detoxify the liver, and will help to put your body back into balance.
- Turquoise is a wonderful colour to boost the immune system and ease inflammation.
- Purple clothing can help heal infections.
- Gold is a good colour to soothe arthritis, rheumatism and back problems.
- Wearing any item of yellow works well for all skin disorders.
- Red increases the heart rate and releases adrenaline (so not good for high blood pressure), and will give you a physical boost and a pickup.
- Wearing blue aids insomnia, asthma, and will bring down high blood pressure.
- Orange is great to help with all digestive ailments.

Whatever emotional or physical challenges you face, colour can act in a therapeutic way to make you feel balanced and happy, and can also make you look healthy and attractive. Just mindfully choose the ones that work for you at any given time, and enjoy the naturally transformational properties of colour.

Chapter 3

Discover How To Mindfully Choose Your Colours... *and dress for optimum well-being*

The best colour in the world is the one that looks good on you.
Coco Chanel

In this chapter I can show you how to find the colours that make you look your best and feel fabulous too. The ones that you will want to embrace into your life and your wardrobe at great speed, heading straight for the shops!

Why is it that on some days people tell you how well you look in a specific colour, and yet on other days you feel completely invisible? Why do certain colours make you feel happy and confident whilst others tired, drained and exhausted?

It's actually very simple. Colour is light which is vital for survival, and light is energy. Each colour has a wavelength of light and colour that will benefit you in different ways. For instance the long wavelengths of red and orange are warm and stimulating, and the shorter ones of blue and violet are cool and calming.

One of the ways you receive colour and light is through your eyes, primarily via the pupil then the lens where it goes to the back of your eye, known as the retina which consists of light sensors, or cones and photoreceptors. These respond to the three primary colours of red, blue and yellow. This transmits approximately 80% of the stimulus to the back of your brain and the visual cortex for sight, where these three colours become a range of varied ones. The other 20% stimulates the glands, i.e. the hypothalamus, pituitary and pineal, which in turn affect your hormonal system and your emotional senses.

Your body needs light, and when you are deprived of it like in the winter months it can sometimes cause a depression like SAD (Seasonal Affective Disorder). Russell Foster is a Professor of Circadian Neuroscience at Oxford University who has spent many years researching the effects of light and dark on our well-being, and especially how our internal clock is fine-tuned to activity and rest, which is directly linked to day and night.

He discovered that we all have a light sensor within the eye, aside from photoreceptors. What this means is that even blind people who have an unconscious awareness of light will be affected by night and day, light and dark.

You need a sufficient amount of light to regulate your sleep and rest rhythms whatever your state of health, young or old. The more balance you get the better your brain functions along with your cognitive behaviour. In short, everyone needs lots of light and colour. As well as seeing colours through your eyes, you also absorb colours through your skin and your own personal aura (the energy field that surrounds every living being). Certain colours you choose to wear can make you radiate with health and well-being, and give you the WOW factor, by putting the life back into fading looks, lifting your spirits and physically balancing hormones whilst boosting your emotions.

I have been privileged to work with many people over the years, helping them to understand how certain colours can make them look and feel their best. It is such a joy for me to see the positive benefits when a shade that resonates with someone's own inherited colouring and personality is placed on them. It becomes very clear which are harmonious, and those that are ageing, draining and ill making. These changes can be very powerful and felt at a deep emotional level.

Helen Kendall-Tobias, a personal colour and style consultant, says, "I've seen quite visceral reactions to colour from some clients, one lady who almost shook as soon as a black drape was placed near to her. For other clients I've seen them blossom as their natural beauty is enhanced in colours from their best colour palette. Others marvel at the effect a colour has on their appearance – often a colour they have not considered wearing before."

Whilst wearing colours you love can make you feel visible in a positive way, there might be some that make you want to run for the hills, perhaps due to bad memories associated with them. Maybe something in your past affected the way you feel and now you don't like to wear any clothing associated with it. I had a client who was bullied at school and, as she wore a green uniform, now refuses to have anything to do with any shade of green such is the strength of her dislike of the colour.

It was the great philosopher Johann Wolfgang Goethe in the late 18th century who believed that colour had an immediate effect on our emotions. In the early 20th century, Max Lüscher a professor of psychology from Switzerland measured people's preferences for chosen colours and how they related to their personality traits. He used this knowledge to treat physical and psychological conditions which provided us with a scientific basis for understanding the power of colour today.

The American art historian Faber Birren who died in 1988 wrote many books about the credible link between psychology and colour. He was consulted by the Army, Navy, hospitals and factories to advise on colour schemes that would enhance productivity. He was particularly interested in the therapeutic properties of bright colours on mental patients. Chosen colours are now being used commercially all over the world, as their impact on office workers, in banks, airlines and even in prisons has been well documented.

Like everything in life, balance is the important factor. If you go overboard on a certain colour, it can end up being too dominant. Look at the colours of the UK's main political parties, blue and red. Blue is the colour of communication, clarity, trust, and reliability, but too much can be self-righteous. Red is powerful, dynamic, driven and gets the job done, but again, too much can be aggressive and bullying. You will need to work with the colours that inspire you, make you feel confident and look fabulous, by keeping them in balance.

A client in her 40s came to see me to have her colours analysed because she had been going through a period of intense change after a divorce. She had trouble moving forward and found herself wearing a lot of brown. This was not a colour she had ever particularly liked in the past, having only accents of it in her wardrobe, but, since her divorce, had felt fixed in her ideas and unable to get motivated after such an emotionally draining experience.

Brown is the colour of stability, something she needed after such an unsettling period; however, it was also a colour that was holding her back, keeping her where she felt safest. It was not encouraging her to move forward. She did not feel particularly pretty or approachable, but she did feel ready for change. So, I put her in shades to suit her colouring of orange for sociability and confidence, and turquoise for youthfulness and fun, adding small accents of brown which harmonised with these colours, ensuring things happened slowly but positively. She contacted me a month later to say she had embraced the new colours and had not only got herself a job, but met some new friends too.

This is a good example of how powerful colours can be, and how important it is to keep them in balance for whatever your emotional needs are at a certain time. Let me ask you some questions about colours and how you feel about them.

Which colour is your favourite and why? Orange is currently mine as it makes me feel confident and happy, and I tend to get complimented in it because it is one of my harmonising colours.

However, I know that I can't wear too much of a good thing as an excess of orange makes me prone to hyperactivity due to its stimulating properties, so I have to balance what I wear with blue, orange's complementary colour and a calming one. An orange shirt or jacket with blue jeans is a perfect balance for me.

Do you wear a lot of black? If the answer is yes then you are not alone! It is a colour many people particularly women have a passion for, believing it to be slimming, easy, chic, and elegant. Whilst it can be all of these things it can also be incredibly detrimental to one's looks; draining and ageing the face by highlighting all the negatives – wrinkles, lines and dark shadows under the chin and around the eyes to name a few. As a result, I stay away from black except for trousers in the winter because I am one of those people it ages dramatically when near my face. Are you also one of these people that shouldn't wear black against your face?

Do you know which colour vibrations will help you? Every colour has its own wavelength that you may need at a certain time for the qualities it can provide you with. If you can tap into the emotion that you are experiencing then you can consciously choose a colour that will help you, rather than randomly picking one from your wardrobe.

Do you know what impression you are trying to make? Plan your wardrobe accordingly because colours reflect your personality, the message you are portraying and how you communicate your feelings.

Do you know what colours to wear that will make you look your best and most youthful as you tackle the ageing process? The ones that will have a positive effect on your face and make your skin tone look even and attractive, highlighting your cheekbones and making your eyes sparkle, bringing out your features and negating the signs of ageing?

The best way to find the answers to these questions is to do the colour draping test that follows and discover which colours have a positive effect on your face and which ones to avoid. Classifying yourself into a colour palette and a season of warm or cool will be very helpful for your new wardrobe, and once you have done the colour draping test, read on to see which colour season you fall into. Then you can choose those colours that will have positive emotional, psychological and physical benefits for you. Think how great that could be: looking and feeling attractive and fabulous, and finding yourself more balanced and happier too! Mindfully choosing your colours will become easy and pleasurable.

Top tips for discovering your skin tone

Colour analysis has been around for over 60 years and is mainly based on the four seasons concept, showing the natural colour groups that harmonise with the four basic skin types. The scientific basis for discovering which colours look fabulous on you is all about finding out what your basic underlying skin tone is.

The three pigments of the skin that give you your skin tone colour are melanin, the brown tones; carotene, the yellow skin tones; and haemoglobin, which gives skin its pink and red hues. One of these pigments may dominate your skin, for example rosy cheeks are a sign of high haemoglobin, or maybe you have a combination of all three pigments. It is true that skin fades as we age, but your underlying skin tone remains the same as it is genetic. The key is to use different shades of your own colours, perhaps not as strong or bright as you would have done when you were younger. Tempering these shades to suit your complexion and hair colouring as you change is important.

The mistake often made by older people with warm skin tones is going into cool shades when their hair goes grey or white, possibly to match it. What they don't realise is that their hair then becomes the focus along with their clothes rather than their face. You may notice that when you have a suntan you can wear stronger colours. Your skin tone hasn't changed for the summer or that specific holiday, you still have the same skin tone underneath, but in a darker hue for that period of time. Also when you go through a period of ill health you may notice that your complexion gets very pale and washed out. Even after a cold the skin can suffer terribly. In this case it is even more important to get the right colours up against your skin as you will, of course, feel better when you see yourself looking better. So, which skin tone do you have?

Do you have a cool skin tone?

Do you have a blue/pink undertone? Then you could be either a summer or a winter seasonal type. If you have a summer complexion then it will be light and rather colourless although occasionally may be slightly darker. Your skin never has a 'high rosy cheek colour' and looks best in pastel shades. Being generally pale and fine textured, your complexion does not tan well but if you do then your skin can take on a rather grey look. Dark colours including black are much too strong for you and your delicate complexion, and will highlight any dark, negative things on your face.

If you have a winter cool complexion you can either be light or dark skinned and not as translucent as the summer skin. Like cool summer you do not have any high colour on your face (not to be mistaken for veins). As a winter you may have an unusual and often distinctive look to your appearance, and whilst pastel shades suit summers they tend to be too pale for most winters, as you will look fabulous in black without showing any signs of darkness on your face. This is the key difference between the two cool skin tones.

Do you have a warm skin tone?

Do you have either a yellow/gold or bronze undertone? Then you could be a spring or an autumn seasonal type. If you have a spring complexion you could have an underlying yellow or gold skin tone and you may well have a tendency to blush easily or have a high rosy cheek colour.

Spring complexions have a great deal of variety and you might be very fair skinned (and often mistaken for the pale summer complexion but will look awful in cool pastels) or be red haired and freckled (does not tan well) or dark with skin that generally tans well with a lovely gold colour. If, however, you have more of an autumn complexion whilst having similar gold undertones you will have a more bronze appearance to your complexion. Your skin tone will differ from spring in that you never have a rosy cheek colour.

Warm skins (with whatever hair colour) do not look good with black up against the face. It has the negative effect of flattening out the warm skin colour, making it look drained and unhealthy, highlighting dark shadows, lines and wrinkles. Basically it ages the face, in some cases more dramatically than others, and these effects worsen with age.

Do you have a dark skin tone?

If you are darker skinned with African, West Indian, Asian, Oriental or Latin tones, you may be able to wear darker shades of colours in your clothing (and make-up for women); however, when black is draped against your face it will determine whether you can wear it well. Your darker skin tone will show exactly the same effects as lighter tones when black is worn up against the face. Being darker skinned you may not automatically fall into the winter season and it could be that you fall into the warm seasonal palette. The colour draping test should help you to see (or ask a friend or relative to help you) which shades suit you best.

Top tips for the colour draping test

What you are looking for are the changes to your skin tone, which will determine your season and what colours suit you best. Please take as little notice as possible of the drape/colour itself and concentrate on your face, as you will see more. A shade that is harmonious to your skin tone will also bring out the natural highlights in your eyes and hair, and you will be able to see the effects for yourself. Your hair and eye colour will come perfectly into harmony when the right colour is against your skin.

The best areas to concentrate on whilst draping are around the eyes and mouth. This is where the skin tone is generally uneven with patches of light or dark colouring. The eye socket area is really helpful too as you can see the whole area sinking in with a poor colour, and also darkness will appear in the corner of the eye. This effect is ageing and draws the eyes together, sometimes making a prominent nose seem to stick out further. These areas will be much less noticeable in the right colours as will blemishes, scars, facial lines, or unattractive features that you would like to draw attention away from.

What you want to see is an even, harmonious, natural tone to the complexion. The colour should not make you look washed out, white and patchy, red and blotchy, or sallow, grey, old and tired. You are looking for a reduction in blemishes and lines, if you have any, and a lifting of wrinkles or dark areas under the chin or the eyes.

You will need:

- A mirror large enough to see yourself from the waist up.
- Lighting that is as bright and natural as possible. If you must be in artificial light then use fluorescent bulbs.
- To be against a background that is plain and colourless.
- For women to remove all make-up. You need a clean face so get every bit off, especially lip colour and eye shadow.
- To be clear of all jewellery round your neck.
- To keep your glasses on (if you wear them) so you can see yourself clearly.
- Black, Cream and White material followed by colour material (a piece of clothing or sheet big enough to put over your shoulders so that there is a large area of cloth under your chin).

How to colour drape:

- Rest your eyes – don't strain them – ignore the material as much as possible and focus on your face.
- Ignore your hair – if necessary pull it off your face with clips or a headband. You need to be free to look at your skin tone.
- Position the colour drape over your shoulders directly under your chin, and make sure it is reflected up on to your face.
- The drape will have a positive or negative effect on your complexion and this will be noticeable immediately.

What happens?

What you don't want to see

- Your skin looking grey
- Your skin looking blotchy and pink bringing out a high cheek colour
- Any unflattering feature being highlighted on your face, i.e. a large nose or jawline
- Your lines or wrinkles suddenly beginning to stand out
- A 'moustache' effect developing above your lip
- Your eyes looking dark and sunken
- Your eyebrows becoming too imposing
- Your lips looking unnaturally dark
- Your roots standing out if you have highlighted hair

What you do want to see

- An absence of dark lines under the chin
- No shadows around the eyes
- The lines and wrinkles having been lifted
- Your skin looking even
- An enhancement of the under eye socket area and inner corner of the eye

- An absence of dark lines under the chin
- A clear and healthy complexion

The effect black has on your skin

Everyone, me included, has different areas that bother us. Please be careful with black, it can be seriously detrimental to the complexion. If you have just discovered that black is a colour that ages and drains your skin then you need to know there are also other colours with black in them that you will need to keep away from your face. Navy blue is one such colour. Many men and women switch to navy as they believe it to be kinder on the skin. Sadly this is not the case as navy can have black in it. So do a lot of dark greens, browns and greys.

If you have any doubt whether you can wear these other colours well, do the self-test in this chapter for the dark colours and you will see what effects they have on your skin. If they highlight the same negatives as black then simply adjust your wardrobe to wear them in the right way for you.

The effect white has on your skin

Watch carefully the difference between white and cream. When you drape white fabric under your chin, it could wash you out and make you look pasty, particularly under the eyes and around the mouth area where the skin tone is usually uneven. The white could make your skin look blotchy as it searches for cool white as an underlying tone in your complexion. In the winter time and as you age you may notice that your skin tone goes paler, and white may well become a colour you used to be able to wear but now only works with a suntan! If white doesn't agree with you then you will notice your face appearing lifeless and stark. It could also highlight any pink areas of acne, broken veins, eczema, or blushing on the cheeks. None of these want to be encouraged; in fact you want to be able to use colour to deflect the effects.

In this instance steer clear of white and all pastel shades that have white as their tinted base (i.e. the summer colour palette). On very dark Asian and African skins, white against the skin could throw an ashy or chalky colour on to the whole complexion as if the skin has been dusted with powder. White causes these effects particularly on warm skin because it throws up on the face a colour that is out of harmony with the underlying yellow/golden based skin tones. If you have a very cool skin tone, white is an acceptable colour against your face.

The effect cream has on your skin

To those of you with warm skins, once you have draped yourself in cream it will highlight just how lifeless and stark white made you look. If you do have a warm skin then cream will automatically give you an even and warm glow. You should instantly look healthier. If, however, you have a very cool skin cream could make you look sallow, and white will be better for you. Cream is a very difficult colour to buy as high street shops always seem to favour bright white which doesn't suit a lot of people and particularly men looking for shirts to wear to work, so if you find one in cream or ivory/off-white buy several!

The effect the other colours have on your skin

Top tips for wearing RED

- For warm skins, bright scarlet red will suit you if you are a spring.
- The more orange, rust colour reds will suit you if you are an autumn.
- If you are a summer you may not like red at all and find it too strong for your colouring. A raspberry pink red will be better suited for your complexion.
- If you have the winter complexion then maroon and burgundy are best.

Top tips for wearing YELLOW

- If you are a spring then golden yellow can look fabulous on you. It will also bring out golden lights in your hair.
- The autumn mustard yellow is a devastating colour on the other seasons, but looks amazing on the golden, bronze skin tone of the autumn.
- If you have either the cool skin tone of the summer or winter, yellow will not be your best colour because your skin base is blue-pink, so it is not naturally harmonising. However, pastel yellow can look great on pale summer skins and the acid yellow very striking on a cool winter complexion.

Top tips for wearing GREEN

- Bright lime green belongs to springs. Green is also THE best colour to wear to counteract the effects of a high pink/red cheek or flushing/blushing.
- Pale mint looks lovely and delicate on the summer skin.
- Olive and khaki green look beautiful on autumn skins.
- Beware dark bottle green unless you have a winter cool complexion as it is a shade with a hint of black. Emerald is also a great colour for you.

Top tips for wearing BROWN

- If you are a spring then brown won't be your favourite colour although you do look good in camel and tan, and these are important neutrals for your bright palette.
- If you are an autumn then you can indulge in most browns with chestnut being your best shade and chocolate brown a good substitute for black.
- For the summer soft rose beige is a great neutral choice.
- Winter complexions suit very dark brown, which has black added to it.

Top tips for wearing PINK

- Whilst peach tones are your best pink, some springs may prefer winter's fuchsia/magenta because you like bright colours, and this can be worn well unless you have a high spring cheek colour.
- Autumn does not have a pink as your skin is bronze based. It is only the salmons and corals that veer towards orange that will bring out the best of your complexion.
- Soft pastel pink is gorgeous if you are a summer.
- Fuchsia and magenta look fabulous on winter skins.

Top tips for wearing BLUE

- Bright and clear blue suits you if you are a spring, as well as turquoise and aqua.
- Air force blue and teal are stunning on autumn skins.
- Blue is as flexible for cool skin tones as yellow is for warm. Pastel blue suits the summer complexion.
- Navy is a harmonious colour for winter skin as well as electric and cobalt blue.

Mindful colour tips for a glowing spring complexion

So let's try and be clear about what the spring complexion is like and if it relates to you. The basis to your underlying skin tone is warmth and a yellow/golden base, and you could have either a very dark look to your skin or a very pale one, often belonging to redheads. One of the main elements to your complexion is a tendency to blush when excited, embarrassed or have had a drink or two! This might have developed into broken veins if you are showing signs of ageing. Most spring skins apart from the very pale and redheaded or freckly variety will tan a golden colour.

If you are a spring your eye colour will probably be blue, blue-green, grey or grey-green, and you might notice if you look close up that you have a yellow sunburst pattern around your iris. However, you could have brown eyes which is more unusual and

41

often applies to Asians who have the spring skin tone with black hair.

On the subject of hair, if you are indeed a spring then yours could be any colour, from a redhead spring and strawberry blonde to the very dark brown and black-haired spring. What is key is that if you choose to colour your hair please make sure you always keep to warm golden or chestnut dye or highlights, and never any cool, ash tones which will simply wash out your warm complexion.

You might feel confused if you have a very pale complexion and are not sure if you fall into the spring or summer category. If this is the case, please do the colour draping test and put cool (pink) shades against your skin and see if you look 'hospital' bed washed out. Compare a pale cool shade of a colour with a brighter version (of orange or coral) and see the difference. When you are wearing the best spring colours up against your skin it will have a healthy glow and a youthful appearance, with a gorgeous vibrant quality, and will harmonise with the warmth of your own personal colouring.

Mindfully choose your best spring colours

If you are a spring then your best mindful colour choices are pure, rainbow colours which will highlight your bright and sociable nature. When we enter the season of spring, it is so joyous to see all the beautiful colours of the yellow daffodils, multicoloured tulips and the bright green shoots appearing on the trees. These encompass your own wardrobe palette.

With the three primary colours of red, blue and yellow spring shades these all get combined to form your fabulous warm greens, corals and purple too. With this mixture you end up with many flattering variations particularly of peach, apricot and coral, which have wonderful harmonies with your underlying skin tone to make your complexion look particularly glowing and healthy wearing these shades of orange in clothing and make-up too.

Whether you have the lighter spring skin or a darker tone, it is important to try and experiment with your bright, warm shades as these will really brighten up your face and make you feel happy too. If you feel 'scared' of wearing bright colours and they are new to your wardrobe, my suggestion is to purchase an affordable top or T-shirt and wear it with your darker neutrals to see how you feel about it and how many compliments you receive, then you can splash out with a more expensive purchase; it ends up being one of your mindful colour choices.

So, to conclude your best colours are clear, warm and bright, and you can also wear pastel versions if you ensure they remain warm and not cool. Sadly, however, black cannot be added because it makes them too dark; and as most spring ladies love to wear black but really it isn't a part of the spring palette, be consciously aware about keeping black and other dark colours away from your face. Remember also having a warm complexion that cream will be much kinder to your complexion than white, which could make you look blotchy and pale. Camel and mid-grey are fabulous neutral colours to combine with your brighter shades.

Spring wardrobe colours to make you look great

Your best wardrobe colours to make you look great everyday are warm and bright and in shades of green, scarlet red, hot pink, coral, blue, yellow and orange. Your neutral shades are gold, off-white, cream, beige and stone. Tan can look fabulous teamed with cream, red, blue-green, peach, coral and yellow. Navy or mid-grey tones are your best choices for jackets, coats and outerwear, and look great teamed with peach, red, bright green, blue-green, coral and yellow.

Spring work colours to make you look great

For those of you who work consider combining off-white or

cream with small amounts of your bright spring colour palette. Ivory or cream also looks great with tan, camel, grey and navy blue. Navy blue, grey, camel or stone are all professional colours and the best choices for work suits.

Spring accessory colours to make you look great

Accessories such as shoes, handbags/briefcases and belts will all combine brilliantly with your palette of wardrobe colours if you buy them in tan, camel, grey and off-white/cream. If you have very dark hair then harmonising with black accessories will work well for you, otherwise avoid. Gold bags and shoes look great for evening wear and your scarves should be bright and vibrant, like you!

Spring jewellery colours to make you look great

As you have the yellow/golden skin tone then your best jewellery will be the bright yellow golds. If you opt for coloured gems then consider the bright blues, reds and greens, and turquoise is a beautiful stone to suit your colouring. If you choose classic pearls then make sure they are oyster tinted.

Mindful colour tips for a beautiful autumn look

As an autumn your complexion will generally appear to be rich and have an almost metallic sheen to it and this is the case whether your skin tone is light or dark. For autumn women if you like a stronger, richer made-up look, then go for it! You can wear a lot of make-up without looking overdone. Your complexion probably tans well and quite dark too, and whilst you also have a gold undertone like the spring complexion the main difference between the two seasonal types is that yours appears more bronze/orange based and you do not have a high cheek colour – ever!

Your eye colour can vary as an autumn and the fairer skinned can have light blue, green, grey-green eyes. However, your eyes will probably be darker brown or green with brown and gold flecks in them if your skin is dark. Autumn seasonal types may have a sunburst effect around the iris; if you look closely enough you should be able to see this. Your hair is likely to be auburn, dark blonde or very dark brown and possibly black. When dying or highlighting your hair be very careful to avoid all the cool tones, and always maintain gold or copper tones whether going lighter or darker. When we enter the season of autumn the beautiful earth tones we see come alive in rich shades of gold, orange, rust, olive greens and browns. Your wardrobe shades are all a combination of these. Like spring, black is NOT in your colour range, so learn to wear it well away from your face if you choose to wear it with your warm autumn colours to allow them to bring out the best of your glorious complexion.

Mindfully choose your best autumn colours

Your best mindful colour choices are warm, earthy and muted just like the autumnal season in nature. These colours also highlight your outgoing and driving energy. Your palette is full of brown shades that can be worn up against your face, unlike the spring season, which gives you a fabulous base of colour (aside from black, not in your range) to combine beautifully your autumn colours of gold, burnt orange, olive and khaki green, teal, air force blue and rich purple.

Whilst you can also wear similar shades of corals with the spring, your shades will be deeper and more muted. Spring has bright orange and for you burnt orange will bring out the more bronze undertone of your complexion much better. You are the only season that looks fabulous in mustard yellow.

Autumn wardrobe colours to make you look great

Your best wardrobe colours to make you look and feel great everyday are orange, red-orange, olive green, gold, dark turquoise, off-white, brown, mustard, teal, cream and of course you have these shades in pastels too. You have so many warm, rich shades of brown to choose from, as well as khaki and warm grey which can be used as strong background neutrals combined with your other brighter colours. Metallic gold and bronze are fabulous fashion fabrics that can be worn at any time but particularly in the evening as a black substitute. They will make you shine and look wonderfully youthful and radiant.

Autumn work colours to make you look great

For the autumn working wardrobe the neutral warm, muted browns are great for business, as well as air force blue, or petrol grey. Combine these with small amounts of your brighter warmer colours, greens, orange, teal, and rust, burnt orange or cream for a formal look.

Autumn accessory colours to make you look great

All shoes, bags/briefcases and belts in brown tones will complement your wardrobe. Black or white are not in your colour range so wear chocolate brown or off-white instead. Gold and bronze accessories are great for evening wear. Wear scarves that complement your warm, muted palette of colours, anything with an edge of drama or a sporty look. You suit tweeds, and paisley prints along with leopard and animal prints too.

Autumn jewellery colours to make you look great

Your best jewellery to complement your skin tone is bronze, copper and antique gold. If you have grey hair then silver is OK, but whatever you choose to wear your jewellery should be bold and chunky and your gemstones can be any size but large ones in amber colours or green are stunning on you.

Mindful colour tips for a healthy summer skin

Understanding that you belong to the summer seasonal palette and do not get confused about perhaps being a spring instead means that your complexion will probably be fairly colourless and although you might have a general pinkness on your face, you will definitely not blush or flush like the spring skin. The other difference is that you do not tend to tan well.

Your underlying cool pink skin base needs light, cool pastel shades to give it a glow and a fresh, even tone to it. As you tend to have pale skin, using these colours up against your face should give you a well needed colour boost and make your cheeks look rosy and healthy. Your hair colour could vary from blonde to brunette and whilst it would be unusual for you to have very dark hair, it can happen, but rarely. Your eyes are probably blue but you will notice a cool, white overlay if you look closely enough. As your colouring demands light, soft shades, please be aware that black is not in your palette. Really dark colours do not suit you.

Mindfully choose your best summer colours

Your best mindful colour choices are light, cool and delicate. When we get to the summer season it's as if all the colours of spring have had a tint of white powder scattered everywhere to give them their pastel, cool look. The summer pastel shades are very soft and pale which will harmonise with your own natural colouring. You will feel very at ease in the beautiful cool shades of blue, and you also have the healing colour magenta in your palette which is a stunning pink, and as you don't tend to opt for red then the cool pinks work well in your wardrobe.

Summer wardrobe colours to make you look great

For all summers you suit the pastel shades of blue, pink and lavender best, followed by light green and some yellow. Navy is a very good neutral colour for you as black is not part of your palette. You can wear dark blues and greys with pink, pale blue, aqua, light turquoise, silver-grey and lilac. Your delicacy lends itself to wearing the currently very fashionable floral designs, which look flattering in pastel shades on a white background.

Summer work colours to make you look great

In business you don't like to be the centre of attention, so cool, pale brown or grey are conservative but professional colours for work that you will feel comfortable in. You can mix these with off-white or one of your coloured pastels, navy or light blue to make you look and feel great.

Summer accessory colours to make you look great

For your accessories, such as shoes, bags/briefcases and belts, these will all look good in browns that are cool and therefore not yellow based. As black is not part of your palette and is very harsh for your colouring please use greys and blues, particularly navy. Choosing to wear scarves in your summer pastel shades will be very complementary up against your face, particularly if you like to wear a background of neutral shades.

Summer jewellery colours to make you look great

With your pale skin tone you will look really beautiful wearing pearls that have a pink tint. All summers can enjoy looking fabulous in platinum, white or rose gold, and choose gemstones in pastel colours of blue, pink and purple.

Mindful colour tips for a striking winter appearance

If you think you belong to the very cool and dramatic winter colour palette then please remember that you will not ever have a high pink/red cheek colour and you don't blush and rarely suntan! You will, however, have a very cool complexion, with rose undertones and your skin could be light or dark. The reason I highlight these misconceptions is that I have seen so many people who have been colour analysed 'winters' but have not been happy with this palette because in fact it has turned out to be incorrect.

The true test for clarification that black is definitely one of your best mindful colours will be to carry out my colour draping. When you put black up against your face this should not highlight negative areas: dark lines under the chin, shadows round the eyes and any lines on the face. Also it shouldn't drain your complexion or make you look washed out, grey or unhealthy.

Your winter seasonal eye colour can be cool grey, blue or combinations of grey and blue, or dark brown, although usually not green. Your hair is likely to be very dark brown, black or white blonde. Luckily for you grey and white hair is very flattering as you age.

Mindfully choose your best winter colours

Your best mindful colour choices include black as you are the only season that can wear this colour up against your face and look fabulous without showing any detrimental signs of ageing or looking washed out. Winter is a season of stark contrasts and it is this dramatic background of white and black that allows you to combine your primary red, blue, yellow with pure green and look really striking, along with fuchsia pink. What could be very helpful for creating your mindful wardrobe is to limit your colour choices on any one day to two! It is your unusual cool skin tone and dramatic hair colouring that enables you to keep things simple and classic, a totally gorgeous look for you.

Think of your palette in terms of icy pastels too, particularly in the cool pink and blue tones. Neon yellow is a great statement colour for you and can be worn in the warmer months, but if it's elegance you desire then opt for dark green or royal blue. Dark grey is a great neutral for you alongside black and dark brown.

Winter wardrobe colours to make you look great

Your best look is dramatic, cool and strong, and the best wardrobe colours to make you look great everyday are white, black, fuchsia pink, neon yellow, electric blue, turquoise, burgundy, plum, deep purple and dark emerald green.

Winter work colours to make you look great

For working winters it's the professional, simple look all the way: black, dark grey, navy blue, dark green along with the contrast of crisp white shirts.

Winter accessory colours to make you look great

Your best mindful accessory colour is simple: black! Grey, dark brown and white are also fab for shoes and bags/briefcases and belts, which are easy to coordinate with your wardrobe. Silver shoes and bags for women in the evening look stunning. For your scarves choose striking patterns: geometric, striped or anything dramatic, in colours that are strong and cool, and look fabulous with your black clothing.

Winter jewellery colours to make you look great

Your jewellery needs to be perfect and minimal. Wear your best metal of platinum, white gold and silver with your best coloured gemstones being diamonds, emeralds and sapphires.

Mindful ways to wear colours that are NOT in your range... and still look fabulous

OK, so you have done all the self-testing in this chapter and have hopefully discovered what your best colours are to help you look young and healthy, and feel great. However, it's realistic to assume that there may be colours that you simply love but they don't fall into your colour palette.

It may well be that black is one of these colours, and if it is then you are not alone! Many people particularly women love to wear it as a colour they feel most comfortable in, to hide any weight issues, to feel chic and elegant in, or simply because it's an easy option. Whether you find black or any other shade of colour detrimental to your looks, here are my top tips on how to wear them and stay looking great:

1   Avoid polo necks in black or a colour that doesn't suit you.

2   If you have jackets or suits in the wrong colour in your wardrobe but they fit you well, you will want to continue wearing them, so place a good coloured shirt (or tie for men) under them so that the collar is the closest thing to your face.

3   Any new jacket that you purchase should be in a colour of your seasonal palette. A blazer in a shade that suits you is a fantastic wardrobe staple for everyone and is highly versatile.

4   Black and dark colours can be really flattering when worn as separates from the waist down, i.e. trousers and skirts particularly if trying to camouflage large thighs or short legs. Team with tops/shirts/jumpers in your favourite colours.

5   Wear any top in a V or low neckline so that this colour isn't directly reflecting up against your face.

6   Wear scarves in colours that do suit you! Whilst these are mainly an accessory for women, in cooler months men can also enjoy their colour benefits. Scarves are brilliant and affordable accessories to have in your wardrobe and will offset any colour that isn't your best.

7   For women if you are wearing a dress in black or any other dark colour not best suited to your skin type, choose a stole, pashmina or a shawl in a flattering shade to wrap around your shoulders. This will cover a large area under your face and neck.

8   A dress in a two-tone colour will be a great addition to your new wardrobe, making sure it has a good colour for you on the top and a darker or different shade on the

bottom half.

9   If you do wear a colour that doesn't bring out the best of your features, make sure you know what colour make-up does as this will go some way in counteracting the negative effects (see the next chapter of this book).

10   Coloured jewellery in your own seasonal palette is a great way to deflect from any clothing not in your colour range.

Mindful ways to wear colour for a great body shape

Can you relate to the fact that most women wear 15% of their wardrobes 85% of the time? Aside from the odd 'classic' outfit for weddings, birthdays and christenings, what is happening to the majority of wardrobes?

The fact is that most people do not know how to use colours to make the best of their good bits and camouflage the bad – do you? The danger of not knowing is that you end up following fashion and buying the latest trend, whether it suits you or not. If no one compliments you, or you feel uncomfortable in it, then you might only wear it once and then shove it to the back of the wardrobe never to be seen again. You end up with a wardrobe that doesn't harmonise in colour and doesn't work for your lifestyle either. Hence things accumulate that don't get worn and you can end up wearing clothes that make you feel invisible.

This means that many people whilst wanting to look their best end up looking a size or two larger by wearing the wrong clothing for their individual shape. They diet and exercise but the truth is this – everybody's shape is determined by their skeletal structure.

You can change your weight and your muscle tone and your posture, but your body type is actually set and no amount of going to the gym will change your basic structure. So, understanding how to use colour to the best of your advantage can make your body look beautifully in proportion and slimmer.

Recently I was on a television show talking about the importance of understanding your body shape and colours. The girl I had taken on to be my model was called Tilly, who was 19 and gorgeous, slim but lovely and curvy too.

The producer was concerned that the viewers wouldn't be able to relate to her and I think would have preferred if I had chosen someone 'larger'. My point was that even someone young and great looking has hang-ups and if you can address your weak areas (real or imagined) when you become aware of them – however young or old – then you can avoid a lifetime of ill-fitting and unflattering clothes, create a wardrobe that works entirely for you, not to mention the time and money you will save every time you go shopping!

Tilly had a curvy body shape, with a big bust, small waist and a long back with proportionately shorter legs. Her problem was that she permanently tried to hide her curves with baggy tops and badly-fitting jackets and she always wore blocks of dark colours trying not to bring attention to these areas.

So what colours should she have worn to make her body look its best? Tilly works in an office and in her spare time she is a photographer. She wanted to look professional but feel comfortable. I chose two coloured outfits to highlight her best features and the first was a more professional business look. I put her in a single-breasted grey jacket with structured shoulders that did up under the bust – this gave her a beautiful shaped waist whilst highlighting her curves and it totally changed the whole of her body structure. I used a grey jacket because it is a professional colour and voted best for all industries. It signifies the ability to work in a calm and dignified way, and with fair judgement. Grey is also much kinder to the complexion than black.

Underneath the jacket I put her in a cream coloured top, as this was a much softer and warmer colour than white (which is best worn on a winter cool colouring). I also chose a black pencil skirt with black opaque tights and black shoes so that all of her bottom half was in the same dark colour, thereby lengthening her legs.

Wearing black shows you are in control, and have strong leadership abilities and good discipline, all great qualities for the workplace. The final touch was a pink scarf up against her face to make her complexion glow and give her a youthful appearance. Strong pink is a dynamic and compassionate colour that shows you can be of service to others, so it was a wonderful colour of choice for her to wear when photographing people to put them at ease. When asked how she felt she said, "I feel so much more confident because I look better, and now I can see my shape highlighted in the way I really want to be seen."

One of Tilly's 'issues' she felt was her tummy. If you like so many people feel that whether real or imagined this is your issue, the best fix is to wear bottom halves that are flat fronted, and high-waisted in dark shades, especially if you also have a long body and shorter legs, like Tilly. If you want to hide a tummy then wearing a scarf can automatically take the eye to that accessory, particularly if it's in lovely bright colours.

The second outfit I put Tilly in was a simple red dress. I chose a bright red to suit her warm skin tone and dark features and, as red is an ambitious colour that showed her enthusiasm and motivation, it was a perfect colour for her starting out on her career. It also gives energy and confidence, both needed for holding down two jobs.

The chosen dress had a fitted top and a high waist that I finished off with a thin black belt and an A-line skirt. This style made her body look totally in proportion as the skirt of the dress skimmed over her tummy and hips, and being high-waisted, made her body look shorter and legs longer. Tilly said this became one of her favourite outfits, getting many compliments.

So, the key to dressing well is thinking mindfully about which colours suit you best and how to wear them by highlighting the positives and hiding the negatives. This guarantees you will have a wardrobe that is tailored entirely to making you look great at all times. Then you can add in high fashion colours that appear each season, when you know they are right for you.

Mindful ways to wear colour for a slim body shape

Weight problems

Whilst weight issues are currently a problem for everyone, in the UK today it is estimated that one in four women are obese (with a BMI of over 30), and it's calculated that the figure is over 60% in America. It is a fact that women generally have more body fat than men. This is due to a number of factors and the first is biological because an average woman will carry 25% of fat compared to 15% for a man. Then you have the hormonal influence that means fat is converted easier into food, alongside the weightier effects of oestrogen. Women also require fewer calories per pound of body weight than men in a normal day.

Mia Törnblom in her book *Self-Esteem Now!* talks about the relationship women have with their bodies. "There are many women who haven't learned to like themselves and their appearance, and who spend far too much time thinking and talking about dieting and losing weight. If we have low self-esteem it can be difficult to choose which people we prefer to have around us. If you don't have a sense of your own value, you often put up with disloyal friends, unreliable partners, bullying bosses and so on."

Slimmer of year 2013 was 45 year old Kim Freshwater who weighed in at 29 stone at her heaviest. In two and a half years she managed to lose half her body weight to become a size 12. She was quoted as saying, "I only wore black but now my wardrobe's full of every colour. I don't think I realised how unhappy I was until I became as happy as I am now."

On average a woman can put on up to 5 kg of weight during the menopause and this can be stored as fat around the waist.

Recently I saw a client who has just entered the menopause, and had become aware and unhappy with the weight she had gained over the past couple of years, with her tummy being her worst affected area, probably due to the decrease in oestrogen.

However, having discovered her best colours she feels much prettier and she has learnt how to use colour to best effect highlighting the positives, and negating the negatives. This has helped her to become more confident and dress in a sexier way to complement her size, and now never wears black. She has developed such great self-esteem that she is genuinely happy with who she is and wants to wear colours that project her positive body image.

Aside from these worrying female statistics, for all men and women body shape is actually determined by skeletal structure. Therefore you can change your weight, muscle tone and posture, but your basic body type is fixed. No amount of dieting will change your bone structure!

Men have similar issues when it comes to weight and often have little idea how to dress for their shape. Recently when I did a workshop with a corporate company the men all wanted advice on shapes and colours to help them choose their best suits and separates to look slimmer. Generally there is less help for men out there and most are simply scared to ask!

The slimming effects of colour

So how do you feel when you are not at your optimal weight? Do you want to hide away and not be seen, so start wearing dark colours to disappear behind? Even if you are having a 'fat' day, do you immediately opt for the failsafe 'slimming' option of black? Why is it that so many people believe black to be slimming? They think that once in a black outfit they will become invisible, and simply disappear into a crowd.

Women in particular who are conscious of their size feel that black camouflages their lumpy bits and doesn't draw attention to their body issues. This is a strongly held belief system that has been heavily influenced by the media, designers and high street retailers – can they all be wrong? The reality is that black is only truly slimming if it suits your colouring, and this means that you fall into the cool skin tone category of the winter seasonal palette. If you do have these cool looks then you will look fabulous in black, but if you belong to one of the other three seasonal types black may actually add weight. So, beware – you might actually be making yourself look heavier if you are wearing a colour that is not in your own personal colour range.

For years overweight people have preferred to wear black and dark colours to make them look slimmer. This is because of the optical illusions created by colour with brighter, lighter and warmer colours appearing closer when compared to duller, darker and cooler colours. Often it is a lack of confidence that sends them into wearing black in the first place, particularly if weight creeps on over time. As the colours you wear are absorbed through your eyes as well as your skin they have a powerful psychological effect on you. A lot of overweight people feel like hiding away, but black can be detrimental to the skin and drain physical energy too.

If you are one of the many stuck in the black rut you will need to start getting into colours gradually with an understanding of what truly suits you and makes you feel youthful and happy. For instance if you are a warm skinned, sunny person then you will always look your best in bright warm colours, using your darker neutrals of greys, stones and blues rather than black to look slimmer. As black can highlight negative aspects on the face, particularly during the ageing process, it is important to under-stand how colour can make you look slimmer and younger too!

Colour tips for looking slimmer:

- The general colour rule is to use stronger, brighter colours on your best body parts to make them more noticeable.

- Bright and light colours should run up and down the middle part of your body with darker ones on the outside for a wonderful slimming effect.
- Darker shades look best on any badly proportioned or larger areas to make them appear smaller.
- Wear colours from the same harmonious family (i.e. warm or cool). They blend into each other as the eye slides easily over them creating a more slimming effect.
- A one colour outfit with patterned scarf will detract from a large area up to the face.
- Colour coordinate your wardrobe and put your clothes into colour groups, that way you can quickly find outfits you want to wear each day, knowing you will look your best. This also avoids panic buying and then realising you already had something similar buried in the back of your wardrobe.
- Wear red which is a stimulating colour to increase your metabolism.
- Pink is a colour of well-being, and will help you to get in touch with your compassionate side and to learn to love yourself.
- Yellow is the colour of self-esteem so find your inner confidence.
- Green is the colour of harmony so great to keep your body and mind in balance and not overeat.
- Choose blues, greys and browns rather than black as your dark neutral colours.

For all women reading this book the next chapter is especially for you! Now you have discovered how to use your new knowledge mindfully to look fabulous dressed in your colour palette, you will learn how to harmonise these colours with your make-up and hair so that you can look and feel great every day.

Chapter 4

Mindfully Lift Your Face With Colours...
and smile with happiness

Nature gives you the face you have at 20. Life shapes the face you have at 30. But at 50 you get the face you deserve.
Coco Chanel

The first thing I notice when I meet someone is their complexion and I am not alone. Your face reflects how you project yourself, and also how you are feeling emotionally as well as physically. Looking youthful and healthy is not just about the clothes you wear, but also how good your face looks along with your hairstyle and colour. In fact it can make all the difference.

The improvement harmonising cosmetics to your own colouring can make, whether it's a dramatic striking look you are after or a natural one, can be truly transformational. The pleasure you get from seeing your face glowing and pretty is not to be underestimated.

When you wear the correct colours on your face your skin tone should even out, eyes sparkle and cheekbones be enhanced. There is nothing nicer than a gorgeous coloured smile to brighten up everyone's day. In fact wearing the right colours can often improve the shape of your face too.

How do cosmetics make a difference?
Make-up plays a vital role for the complexion at any age, but particularly as your skin starts to show the detrimental signs of ageing. It then becomes more important to camouflage the negative aspects that start to appear.

As the dark shadows, lines, wrinkles and blemishes of age make an unwelcome appearance on your face, the right coloured foundation is key and can be transformational on the ageing skin. It also becomes more important to accentuate your good features, and the right coloured blusher and eye make-up will ensure harmony and a natural look that can make you look younger and healthier.

Equally when you are young as a teenager or in your early twenties, it is of such great benefit to learn about your colours at this age so that you can know how to look your best throughout your life. Also, let's not forgot the fact that it will save you hundreds of pounds on wasted cosmetics!

Mindful make-up tips for the spring colouring

As you are someone who likes change, you are probably the first at the MAC make-up counter every season trying out new looks and colours! The truth is that whilst you can alter your colours along with the seasons, you should always look to wear shades that are bright and vibrant. Your complexion is what is known in the colour analysis world as 'peaches and cream' so your cosmetics need to have a warm undertone in every piece of make-up you now mindfully choose.

Foundations

Your foundation can vary from being very pale to very dark depending on your natural colouring; however, the important thing is to ensure you only ever use a warm toned foundation and one which is yellow/golden based, either peach or beige rather than rose or pink.

Blushers

The best harmonising blusher shades for your 'peaches and cream' complexion therefore should be in peach, apricot or coral, but for older skin you may wish to use a more muted peach-beige if you feel more comfortable in it.

If you have one of the high coloured spring complexions that either blushes easily or you are prone to hot flushing, you will suit blushers that swing more towards the pink end of warm, but make sure you still keep the yellow base. This is often a revelation for women with a high cheek colour or broken veins who have wrongly assumed they have a pink based cool skin tone. Applying peach or orange shades of blusher are the best for blending in a high cheek colour. The results can be truly transformational, as so many women stay clear of any blusher at all due to fear of looking 'even more pink'.

If you are a darker skinned spring woman then the key for you is to simply choose the same warm orange base but go darker, always keeping the brightness there in order to harmonise with your own colouring.

Eyeshadows

For you spring women it might be another revelation to be told that the best colour eyeshadow for your yellow/golden based complexion is in fact 'green'! This is because green has the perfect balance of yellow and blue combined to harmonise with your skin tone. Warm shades of green will create a really beautiful natural effect on your eyes, and not only enhance the colour, but make the whites look really sparkling and clear – give it a try and see for yourself! Otherwise purple eye shadows will look lovely and pretty because of the complementary effect on your peach skin tone, which you could combine with gold for a great evening look.

If you like to wear eyeliners to enhance the shape of your eyes, again choose green, and also you could try the neutral shades of grey but avoid black unless you have very dark features. Browns (unless a light golden colour) should be avoided as they may make your eyes look rather bleary which is not the aim at all!

If you choose to use a highlighter, in order to reflect your eyes in a flattering way you need to consider the lighter shades of peach, cream or soft yellow/gold. Mascaras should be brown, grey (or green for a party look) but if you are a dark-haired spring, you can use black.

Lipsticks

Peachy pink, coral and mango shades are the best colours that will complement your lips and harmonise with the rest of your make-up. Choose the strength that suits your particular colouring; and if you like the bright shades, then go for it, just make sure you pick the warm not cool ones. You can also choose darker, richer more bronze-red colours if you have darker skin.

Make-up colours for business

Golden browns and greys if used lightly will be the best 'neutral' tones for you to wear in combination with your work wardrobe as they generally harmonise with your other neutral clothing colours and also with your brighter ones too.

Mindful make-up tips for the autumn colouring

If you have the autumn colouring then your skin tone will have a lovely warm metallic glow to it and your make-up therefore needs to enhance this, warming it up not cooling it down. This will ensure your complexion looks healthy, even and attractive. Also, you can wear quite a lot of make-up without it looking really obvious or unnatural, even well into old age, so experiment with the right colours that suit you from the ones I recommend below.

Foundations

Whether you are a paler more pastel autumn woman or have a really dark skin tone, you will need to use foundations that have a warm peach and beige colouring. Do not use any pink based foundations; this is really important as these tones will not bring out the best of your complexion and could ruin the overall look of your make-up.

Blushers

The best blushers for you are going to be in the red-brown and golden-brown shades and you could also consider true brown too along with a rich apricot shade as well. The key for you is to ensure the colours are rich and muted, and of course you can go paler if you are a lighter skinned autumn woman.

Eyeshadows

Unlike the spring complexion your eyes look amazing in all shades of browns and also gold as these are really flattering. You can also wear green eyeshadow; however, you look best in the khaki shades and anything with a bronze/gold base to it and also the more teal side of blue/green. If you like purple then the darker warm shades are also within your colour range.

For your choices of eyeliner, brown looks fabulous, and green is also a great option in your khaki range. For highlighters consider gold, light beige and peach and steer clear of white particularly, and only use cream if you are a very fair skinned autumn or it will be too light for you and out of harmony with the rest of your make-up.

Brown mascara really enhances your eyes and would be my first choice as a recommendation; however, you could also wear green and purple too for an evening look. You can wear black mascara but really this is only a good choice if you have extremely dark features.

Lipsticks

Your lip colour needs to harmonise with the rest of your cosmetics to finish off the overall look so choose any shade of brown/bronze, orange and deep warm red too, which especially looks fabulous if you have really dark hair.

Make-up colours for business

At work you can choose to wear brown make-up with small

amounts of other colours such as green, orange and red which will combine well with your muted, earthy based wardrobe.

Mindful make-up tips for the summer colouring

Sometimes it can be hard for summer women to get excited about wearing make-up at all! As you have a natural delicate and often pale colouring, often choosing to wear even a really small amount of cool, pink based colours on your face will make a huge difference to you and make you look healthy and pretty too. For this reason it is really important that any cosmetic you do decide to use must enhance and not overpower you so always remember to keep your make-up light and simple.

Foundations

Due to your soft and often pale complexion it is really important you find a foundation that has a cool, rose pink undertone, rather than peach/coral or orange to highlight your natural colouring. Also ensure that the foundation does not have a heavy look to it; everything you use needs to be light.

Blushers

Again remember you have a cool, pink based skin base, so any shade of soft pink particularly rose shades will make your complexion look healthy and feminine.

Eyeshadows

You need a really delicate light eyeshadow colour that is cool and so any light purple, pastel blue or grey will look lovely on your eyes. If you want to really look dressed up for an evening out then consider pale pastel pink and silver too. For mascara keep away from anything too hard or severe, so black is only advisable if you have very dark hair. Greys and browns are much more flattering on your pale colouring, or you could choose blue too. Any highlighters applied should be in shades of soft pink, cream and silver.

Lipsticks

Just adding a small amount of one of your flattering lipsticks and/or glosses in cool pale pinks, or raspberry even, will be particularly pretty on you.

Make-up colours for business

As summer women often find it hard to wear make-up and it is important to look well groomed for work, consider pale brown and taupe eyeshadows combined with any of your pastel shades of pink/rose lipsticks, which are perfect for most work environments combined with any work outfits in navy or light blue and light grey.

Mindful make-up tips for the winter colouring

If you are a woman with the winter colouring then it is very likely you will be a perfectionist about your image. Your skin tone is very cool and you may also have dramatic features (probably an opal-like complexion with very dark strong features and hair colour). Therefore what you need to bring out the best and harmonise with your skin tone are the strong, dark jewel tones that will automatically make you look more striking.

Foundations

If you definitely have the cool complexion of the winter woman you won't have any high cheek colour (like the spring woman) so you will need foundations with cool, blue undertones, and this goes for those of you with either light or dark skin.

Blushers

As your skin can appear opaque, cool and often colourless, your best blushers are going to be the strong blue-pinks which will give you a healthy look. With your colouring you should be able to wear a lot of make-up and look fabulous, unlike the cool summer woman's lighter, more delicate complexion.

Eyeshadows

For you keeping all aspects of your make-up cool and dramatic is the key, so most shades of blue will be flattering to your eyes and overall look, and wear them strong and bold. You can, however, also choose to use cool strong pinks and purples too. Both your eyeliner and mascara can be either black or grey, and highlighters are best in silver, grey or pale pink.

Lipsticks

The cool strong pinks and reds will have the most stunning effect on the lips and make your overall look really dramatic. Please do, however, keep away from the warm lipstick shades at all costs.

Make-up colours for business

Your neutral wardrobe colours of black, dark grey, navy blue, dark green combined with crisp white shirts provide you with the perfect smart, professional business wardrobe. So your make-up colours can be strong but simple, and enhance your features without overpowering you.

Mindful make-up tips for a natural 'Facelift'

First of all I need to be upfront about the fact that I am not a make-up artist. My skills lie in matching harmonising cosmetics to individual skin tones. I also impart some great tips that I learnt when training many years ago that are simple and easy to apply and make a huge difference to the overall look. My aim is to achieve the natural 'facelift' look by gently creating a lifting effect with coloured make-up.

Few women have the time to spend putting on their make-up in the morning, but equally in my experience there are not many who know what colours suit them and how to put colours on to best effect, highlighting their features and hiding problem areas. I always ask clients to bring their make-up bags with them during a consultation and often end up putting quite a lot in the bin! Once you have the knowledge you can mindfully choose your best colours, and this should actually save you time every day not to mention money on wasted cosmetics.

It's hard not to follow the latest fashion craze for colours, be it clothing or make-up. We all want to look our best, so it's only natural. However, a little bit of knowledge goes a long way, and my aim is to give you some really easy tips to enhance your features and hide any negatives in a quick and effective way. Knowing whether you are a warm skinned spring or autumn woman or a cool summer or winter will help you to choose the colours of your cosmetics in a more targeted way and save you a fortune in the long run whilst also getting you lots of compliments!

When it comes to the make-up part of my consultations I always work on clean skin and in the most natural light possible. As I am in a studio environment I also have colour corrective lighting, but if you are in a shop trying out make-up it's important you get yourself near a window to check how your colours look on your face in a natural light, particularly foundation. The aim is to give your skin an even quality to it, depending on whether you have any problem areas, i.e. a high cheek colour or acne, in which case you may need more coverage.

Foundation is the cosmetic I find women struggle with the most. In the majority of cases, they want a 'natural' look so there is no obvious foundation on the face. In order to find what colour suits you best you will need to blend a small amount of different shades along your jawline. Do not be fooled into thinking putting testers on the back of your hand is going to work as the skin on your face is often not the same colour.

A good colour for you should look harmonious and settle into your skin. You may even have to blend two foundations to get the exact colour. However, the end result is that you should not be able to see a line under your chin once you have applied it to your face. Please note that in most cases foundation should not need to be applied to your neck.

The general rule for finding the right colour foundation is if your skin has either a yellow or golden base to ensure you choose a warm foundation; either peach or beige, light or dark depending on the depth of colour to your skin. If you have a pink based skin tone then your foundation needs to be cool with a pink/rose base.

Tricks for applying foundation

Once you have found the colour that suits you best I find applying it with a sponge will give you the smoothest most even look. Start by applying it to your forehead and then stop and check that the colour is right for you. If it is, then carry on over your entire face making sure you cover your eyelids as well, and go right into the corner of your nose. You know you have got it right when there is no visible foundation colour across your jawline.

If you are applying concealer before your foundation then you can put a dusting of translucent powder over it and touch up with more concealer if needed after the foundation. However, if you choose to disguise dark areas like shadows under the eyes after the foundation then using a lighter shade will help.

If you have any blemishes or other imperfections that you want to hide on your face, then use a concealer shade that is closest to your foundation colour. At this point, having applied foundation and concealer you can choose whether to apply a powder which will seal it all in and ensure it stays on as long as possible, also removing any shine you may experience, particularly if you have oily skin.

OK, so once your base is on and your skin tone looks lovely and even, the next step is to apply *blusher*. I personally always opt for a powder blush as I find it much easier to place exactly where I want it to go. Blusher is a super powerful tool as it shapes and balances your face and really can enhance and flatter your individual shape.

As you age skin starts to droop, and of course everyone has different skin tone and bone structure which makes a difference. The aim with blusher is to firstly find a colour that suits you. If you have a yellow/golden based skin tone, keep to the warm colours of coral and apricots, moving into the reds, oranges and browns if you have a more bronze based complexion. For those of you with a pink undertone, keep to the cool pinks and reds.

Before you begin applying blusher never overload your brush with colour as you can always go back over the area if there isn't enough colour for you. Also during the evening you may want to apply another layer on top of your day look so it should be easy for you to follow the line of your cheekbone.

To get the 'lifted effect' that will be so flattering, start in the centre of your cheekbone and move up and down towards the temples, which will give you a natural cover with no obvious edges. Using colour in this way will not only define your face giving it shape, but will give you a natural facelift appearance. A lot of make-up artists encourage the application of blusher on the apple of the cheek but in my opinion, whilst this might be OK when you are young, it won't highlight your cheekbones or lift them as you age. You can always use two colours for a more glamorous blusher look, always using the lighter shade above the darker along your cheekbones.

Lip colour can be the make or break of an overall look. You can have gorgeous cheeks and eyes but the wrong lipstick shade can make your mouth look small and teeth appear a bad colour. You may have found yourself stuck in a rut and using the same shade for many years. This is great if it is the right shade and you receive compliments on the colour. However, it's always fun to experiment and it might be that whilst the colour you love to wear is good, there might be another shade, slightly lighter, darker, warmer or cooler that looks even better!

If you have a large mouth then you will probably look better in darker shades, but if your mouth is on the small side then it is the lighter ones that will increase the size. If you like to use a lip pencil to enhance the shape of your mouth, it may help you to put foundation or powder as a base to work on first. Whatever you do, the important thing is to try to make your lips look as natural as possible. Your make-up should harmonise with your colouring at all times, going stronger for night time or party use.

If you want to make your lips look bigger, plumper and more youthful then use a touch of pearlised lipstick in the centre of your lips, making sure, however, that you are using the right colours to suit you. If you want to avoid making yourself look older, avoid really dark colours on a small narrow mouth.

If you have a warm complexion then the peaches, corals, apricots, warm reds, oranges and even browns will suit you. However, if you have a cool skin tone then it's the cool, icy pastel pinks that will look fabulous on you as well as cool reds and fuchsia pink.

How to make your eyes stand out

They say that the eyes are the windows to the soul! When your eyes stand out for all the right reasons with the whites looking really clear and sparkling and the colour enhanced you can look really healthy and attractive. Some colours that you put on your eyes, however, may make them look smaller when you want to enlarge them, or can make them look severe by using too much black. Eye make-up should always harmonise with your own colouring, and ensure you are presenting the image that best reflects who you are at any given moment, at home, work or play.

Whatever your eye colour, it is important to use make-up that suits your skin tone as well as the actual colour of your eyes. For instance blue eyeshadow doesn't always look best with blue eyes and often this means your eyes will have to fight for pole position over and above your eyeshadow.

For those with a yellow/golden or warm based skin tone, that have blue eyes, you may well notice if you look carefully into your eyes that you can see a yellow overlay that might appear like a golden sunflower, which in fact makes your eyes sometimes appear green. The pattern of your eyes may be clear without any strong markings. This means that your best eye colours will be all shades of warm green, lighter for pale skins, and darker to tone with dark complexions.

Cool blues will not suit you well, as most shades of brown don't either. Use gold, lavender, and most greens, with black or brown mascara. Eyeliners should be in greens or neutral greys, and try and avoid black unless you have very dark features.

If you have a golden/bronze based complexion with either blue or more likely brown/green eyes and you notice some dark petal shapes in your eyes then you probably suit all the brown eyeshadows, and khaki green will look fabulous on you as well as the darker golds and bronzes. You can also wear purple but keep away from blues unless on the teal/green border. Eyeliners in browns and greens are best and avoid black unless you have very dark colouring.

With a pink based complexion that is fairly colourless you probably have blue eyes and you can wear the muted blues, greys and lavender really well. Softer shades of grey and brown mascara are better for you than black unless you have very dark hair. Highlighters should be in soft pinks and creams, and silver for the evening.

When I apply *eyeshadow* I always first use a light highlighter all over the eye and socket. The reason I do this is because this will create the effect of 'lifting' the eye socket area upwards. It's a wonderful way to use light shadow to full effect. So, for this reason I use a light yellow/golden shade for warm skins, and a silvery white or grey for cool. This is predominantly an evening look but it does mean that you can then apply eyeshadow colour on top of it without your eyes looking really 'made up'. If you are one of those ladies who look fabulous in green then the last thing you will want is a large block of green standing out above your eye.

I always use colour sparingly to start with particularly if trying out a new one for the first time, and my general rule is to put a line of coloured eyeshadow above the eyelashes, then leave a small gap above this on the eye socket (to allow the highlighter to show through) and then put one simple line over the crease of the eye socket. My clients are always really surprised how effective this looks making their eyes really stand out, the whites looking incredibly clear and white without looking like they have a lot of eyeshadow on.

I then put eyeliner in a faint line underneath the eye and on top just to about halfway along the eye to pull it out and make it look bigger (provided you don't have 'prominent' eyes – see below). Finally I put on a layer of mascara in either brown, grey or black depending on the colouring of my client.

Eyebrows are a really important part of balancing your face and also give you an authority which is an important part of dressing well particularly in business, so please take notice of their shape to see if they flatter your face.

You will need to look objectively at your eyebrows to see if they need tidying up. If you have any stray hairs underneath your main line of brow then this can give the impression of your face drooping, so make sure you remove them accordingly, and also any hairs across the centre of your nose will make the face look severe and the eyes too close together. Make sure you choose the shape of your eyebrows to suit your own face and look.

Eyebrow fashions change and currently it's popular to have natural and heavy looking ones. Personally my eyebrows which are blonde started to fade in definition in my late 40s, and I like to use a natural taupe coloured liner pencil to make them look stronger and to help define my face shape which is angular and long. For me it is an invaluable part of my make-up regime, so it's important to decide what suits you best and then work with that.

Colour on your brows needs to be the closest you can match to your own shade, and pencil in any gaps or make them look more noticeable by using an empty mascara brush rather than a pencil. If you have grey eyebrows you may wish to mix colours to find the most flattering but taupe is always a good neutral in this case.

Mindfully choose your best coloured glasses

Glasses have become big fashion accessories, which is great news for us all, young and old. It used to be rather intimidating wearing basic, dull 'specs', but nowadays the choices are endless and wonderfully creative; however, that in itself can prove problematic not knowing which colours and styles to choose. Wearing the right coloured glasses can highlight your features and face shape, whereas the wrong ones can be detrimental to your overall appearance. So here's my advice on a seasonal basis.

Spring colouring suits the warm tones of coral and cream, and if you want to go brighter you can, and choose from bright blues, greens and oranges. Your best metal will be gold and neutrals of light brown, tan, and warm greys, but try and keep away from anything dull and dark, especially black unless you have very dark hair.

Autumn colouring suits the very warm and muted browns and tortoiseshell burnt orange, olive green, and teal. Your best metal is anything golden or bronze based and neutrals of dark brown and camel are best. Avoid blue toned frames.

Summer colouring suits the cool, pastel shades of blues, pinks and purples. Lilac and light grey is also lovely with pearlised shades being light and delicate. Your best metal is rose gold and the pastel shades of grey and mink are very flattering.

Winter is the only seasonal type that can wear black frames really well. You suit the sharp and cool look of black, dark grey, electric blue, fuchsia pink, or white. Your best metal is silver or platinum.

Mindful colour hair tips to dye for!

One of the questions I get asked the most by women is: "What colour should I dye my hair?" Even though the general rule is to go only two shades lighter or darker than your natural colour, many women don't realise it's also about keeping the colour warm or cool along with their natural inherited skin tone. This can really make all the difference.

I see a lot of women who have gone from their natural brown to blonde, but in some cases have gone far too light blonde which only makes their complexion look pale and washed out as a result, which can in turn be very draining and ageing on the complexion. If you have a yellow/golden base skin tone then your hair will always need to have a golden colouring in it, even if only in the highlights.

Women who are very pale and have cool complexions suit the ashy shades of blonde. Equally if you are a brunette and want to warm up your colour, then stick to caramels, coppers and dark golden shades. Redheads of course can look incredibly striking without any help at all and often shouldn't have colours added.

I think we can all notice when women age and start to dye their hair too dark. As the skin ages it goes paler and hair colour should naturally lighten with the complexion, so dying it the shade you used to twenty years ago can in fact make you look even older.

If you want to embrace your natural locks and go grey and white as you age, this can look wonderfully striking particularly if you keep the colours you wear up against your face strong, and not too washed out or pale. The mistake many women make as they age is to match their fading hair colour with their clothes, thereby making their hair stand out too much.

So is your hair your crowning glory? We all have bad hair

days, let's be honest, but generally do you feel your hair enhances your looks or lets you down? In the words of L'Oréal: "Is your colour your signature?"

Your hair reflects how healthy you are, how well you value yourself and what kind of personality you are. Do you have wavy, romantic looking locks, a sharp dramatic bob, or a cool pixie cut? Does your hairstyle suit the shape of your face and is the colour making you look attractive, healthy and youthful, or draining your skin and making you look older, pale or unwell?

You are an individual and you need to consider a colour and style that suits YOU, not Cameron Diaz! I remember many years ago when I was a teenager and Chris Evert was the number one tennis player in the world, and being an avid lover of the sport I thought she was an amazing role model. So I went to a hairdresser and asked for a 'Chris Evert' hairstyle.

Now she happened to have blonde straight thick hair and I had (at the time!) brunette, fine, wavy hair. Her style was a really heavy fringe cut right back way beyond her ears, which no doubt kept her cool on the tennis court. For me, not being a professional tennis player it was a disaster. I looked like I had a pudding bowl stuck on my head and a rather dull brown one at that! So copying celebrities should really only be used as a guideline, and your hairdresser can advise you whether you have the right hair and face shape to suit that style.

For instance, if you have a long face what you require from your hairstyle is width, not height or a long length. However, if you have a wide face, then you definitely need height at the top or a longer length to slim line your face. You really need to work with what you have and your style must be practical for your daily life – if you don't have the time to tong, backcomb and flick your hair, choose an easy style that needs low maintenance.

Andrew Jose is one of the world's leading hair stylists and an acclaimed teacher, who runs his own salon in London, and he says: "A good haircut doesn't just look good when you leave the salon. The things to consider are how it moves when you walk, how easy it is to maintain and keep it looking right. There are many ways to find balance and beauty regardless of face shape. I always try to draw a heart around the face as this perspective brings out great features and when taken into consideration with body shape works really well."

Choosing to colour your hair more naturally to your own colour won't show roots every month, and therefore you will spend less money and time at the hairdresser's. I often advise women to have a few high or lowlights in their hair depending on their skin tone and natural hair colour, as this can beautifully complement the face and add depth and interest to an otherwise flat colour. Tinting your hair if you are going grey will need to be re-done approximately every 6 weeks, so don't start down this path unless you are prepared to keep it up.

Andrew Jose says, "Your hair is fixed by the time you reach early adulthood and will remain that way unless there are changes to health and lifestyle. When you reach middle age grey hair can start appearing as the hair shaft loses pigment, and approaching old age, a woman's hair should remain thick as it was in adulthood unless you experience ill health or you are genetically predisposed. Colour and skin tone are closely linked to how you appear, and getting this right really can make you look and feel good."

Long ago before I became a colour consultant, and when I was naturally brunette, I used to henna my hair which would give it a rich gloss and made my colour look a bit more interesting. However, one day things went badly wrong. You have to remember it was the 80s and perms were all the rage, although what I asked the hairdresser for was a 'body wave', a lovely bouncy slightly wavy look for my shoulder-length hair. What I actually got was a full-on corkscrew version and it really didn't suit me. I had no choice though but to wait till it lost its curl because straightening irons and solutions just didn't exist in those days of crazy perms.

Anyway to make matters seriously worse I put my usual henna on top of my curly top and within 10 minutes noticed a deep black line of hair sticking through the towel. I had gone deep ebony and it looked hideous against my warm skin tone, just awful.

My skin looked so pale I looked anaemic; nothing in my wardrobe worked with my jet black hair the next morning when dressing for work. I ended up wearing all black to try and 'harmonise' with my new Goth appearance, but when I walked through the office door, my boss was so horrified she took all the money she had out of petty cash and told me to go to the nearest hairdresser and get the colour "stripped out" as she said she simply couldn't work with one of the Witches of Eastwick!

I now spend rather a lot of time and effort getting my hair coloured with golden blonde highlights mixed into my brunette natural colour, and keep a layered cut that allows my hair to have some bounce and body to frame and give width to my long face. I envy women who have straight, sleek bobs that look effortless and stay put, but I have to work with what I have and make it the most attractive I can. For me, this involves knowing what suits me and having a really experienced, fabulous hairdresser who understands my needs.

Your hair colour and personality

Hair colour can also say a lot about your personality and how you, as a woman, are perceived in society. For instance, the 'dumb blonde' stigma remains, even though scientists have disproved the theory that blondes are less intelligent and the reality is that only one-fifth of the world's population is in fact naturally blonde!

Blonde hair colour became popular during the Renaissance and was seen as a cultural symbol of angelic qualities. If you are a natural blonde and belong to the world's one-fifth then you are likely to be bright and fun loving and enjoy being the centre of attention, just like your hair colour, and research has proved that blondes (whether real or dyed) do in fact have more fun and are seen as sexier than other hair coloured ladies.

Perhaps you are one of the world's two per cent of natural redheads? The Egyptians all wanted red hair as it was seen as a sign of true beauty and used henna as a dye to get the desired red shade. The redheaded personality has been perceived as fiery, passionate and possibly outspoken. Apparently only 13% of female CESs choose to hire a red-haired candidate. However, these ladies often rise to high ranking positions and make great team leaders, and are creative, energetic people. So, if you are a natural redhead, embrace your stunning hair because colours look so striking on you, particularly shades of green!

If you are naturally in the majority of women who are brunette then please be aware you are considered intelligent, hardworking and sophisticated. Brunettes will be the most likely candidates chosen for job positions even though there is actually no scientific evidence that brown-haired lovelies are smarter than other hair coloured ladies.

On the women's lifestyle site Yahoo Shine there was an article quoting Midge Wilson, PhD, Professor of Psychology at DePaul University, about how hair colour can convey subconscious signals about your career potential. "Though policies on what hairstyles are acceptable in the workplace have loosened, hair can still signify certain levels of professionalism," she says. "If you're in a creative or artsy field where you're required to think outside the box and pay attention to trends, a bold hue can be an asset. Whereas if you have a more serious minded role at work, you may not want a bold, eye-catching (distracting) hair colour."

A poll conducted by Superdrug found that thirty-one per cent of women dyed their hair from blonde to brown to "appear more intelligent" and thirty-eight per cent said being blonde held them back professionally. A quarter claimed to have got promoted after going darker!

So, being dark seems to have a more serious and down to earth appearance. If, however, you have naturally black hair (and are probably either Asian or African), you will be viewed as exotic and mysterious. It was Cleopatra's extraordinary beauty that made black hair so coveted and nowadays raven-haired ladies are viewed as clever, deep thinkers who are also considered good at finance.

Whatever your hair colour, if you have remained your natural colour or chosen to be something different, it is vitally important to feel happy and contented in the knowledge that it is right for your skin tone, your lifestyle and your personality. Whether you have blonde, red, brown or black hair, the colour should make you visible in the way you want to be seen.

Mindfully choose your best hair colour

Warm skin tones

If you have either a yellow/golden spring skin tone (that flushes or blushes easily) and either blue, green or brown eyes that have a clear eye pattern, with no flecks, crypts, lines or dark pockets in them, then you must be aware of keeping your hair a golden warm colour and do NOT go cool or ashy, this will wash you out.

If you have a bronze autumn skin tone and blue, green or brown eyes with an eye pattern like deep petals in them then you need to keep your colours warm and rich. If choosing to go blonde, keep it a dark golden shade and do not go too light as it will make your skin look dull and unhealthy. You can also go a rich chestnut and a dark brown with caramel highlights.

Cool skin tones

If you have a cool, pink based summer skin tone with blue or brown eyes and your eye pattern is similar to cracked glass (and has no yellow in it) then you must keep to the ashy colours, platinum blondes and cool reds, never use warm gold, or bright shades, they always need to be soft and light, and nothing heavy or too dark.

If you have the really cool, blue based winter skin tone (you can possibly see veins under your skin that make it appear blue) and your eye pattern either has deep lines from the centre to the outside or you have deep dark crypts then your colours need to be dramatically cool. You will look fabulous as a platinum blonde, or a really white-haired lady. No golden or warm shades of any colour as you will lose your dramatic quality.

Going grey

So, there is no getting away from the fact that as we age our hair goes grey, or let's call it silver as it sounds nicer! Research tells us that once we have reached over the age of 50 going grey is top of the list of things that make women feel the least confident about their appearance. If you choose to go grey naturally there are ways to do it and stay visible.

The main rule at this time in your life is not to go darker than your own natural colour. If you choose not to remain natural (and grey really does suit a lot of people) then you can consider keeping the natural colour you have been all your life. Otherwise choose a rinse or a tint that is a shade or two lighter than the grey you become. The really important thing to remember when going grey is to get the colour right for your cosmetics, and this will ensure you age beautifully because your skin and hair are in perfect harmony with each other and you!

I am often asked whether skin tone changes as you get older and the answer is NO, it does not. Both your hair and skin will lighten, that's natural, but you do not suddenly change colours; you were born having inherited your genetic colouring, the key thing is to embrace this and use colours that make you visible throughout your life. This will keep you youthful whatever your age.

Chapter 5

Mindfully *Red – Choose your shade of red and feel energised and positive*

Are you looking for a new challenge and want the energy to succeed?
Do you want to make a good impression at a job interview or get promoted and show your drive and enthusiasm?
Are you searching for romance and going on a date or making new friends and want to feel vital and confident?
Are you attending an event and want to radiate health and happiness?
Are you taking exams and need empowerment to keep motivated?
Are you in need of a physical boost or want to slim without dieting?
Are you going through the menopause or the ageing process and need some extra energy?

Getting some red into your life will help you emotionally, physically and psychologically. Before delving into the benefits of wearing red and what shades will suit you best for optimum well-being, let's just have a look at the background to this wonderfully dynamic colour. It will help you to understand a bit about its power and why you may want to choose it as one of your mindful colours.

RED Background

Red is a hot colour being at the warmest end of the colour spectrum, and it is often associated with danger; warning and red stop signs render the strongest reactions when we see them.

Red also demands the most attention and is associated with strength and a drive to action. It signifies new beginnings, and is a friendly, warm colour. It physically stimulates the body because it releases the hormone adrenaline, so will raise your temperature, encourage activity, and stimulate your nervous system. It has the power to give you energy and is a wonderful tonic if you are feeling tired, sad or run-down.

Red will help you to face any fears of the future you may experience, and propel you into action. It is a great colour to embrace if you need to face new challenges, like getting a job, making new friends, or looking to make changes in any area of your life.

Red is one of the three primary colours, along with blue and yellow. If you combine red with blue you get differing shades of purple which will give you the qualities of both of these colours combined, so you get the dynamism of red and the calming element of blue which stops any extremes of temperament. Then if you mix red with yellow you get orange, a warm, sociable and confident colour, the combination of the fire of red and the joy of yellow.

Red has always been associated with courage relating back to the Middle Ages when red was symbolised by the blood of Christ, and the sacrificial aspect of red has been carried on through battles ever since. Red was therefore seen as the colour of war and anger.

A study, by German sports psychologists at the University of Münster which was reported in *New Scientist* magazine, found that people who wear red clothing score on average 10 per cent more in competitions than if they were wearing any other colour. Taking football teams as an example, it could be because red encourages aggressiveness and dominance or that it gives players more confidence.

Scientists at Durham University looked at how colour influences competitiveness in sports and they specifically analysed Olympic boxing, taekwondo and wrestling, and discovered that nearly 55 per cent of bouts were won by the competitor in red.

As the *Telegraph* quoted at the time, "There is now good experimental evidence that red stimuli are perceived as dominant and that they cause negative effects on performance in those viewing them," said Robert Burton, one of the researchers. "It is plausible that wearing red also makes individuals feel more confident, although this hasn't yet been tested."

Red has also been connected with love, passion and romance. Everyone knows that on Valentine's Day it's customary to give a loved one a red rose to symbolise their feelings. However, red is more readily linked to passion and pink to love.

Red is also a ceremonious colour, and we use it today at major events by laying down a red carpet to welcome important people, and in China it is seen as the colour of happiness, celebration and good luck. In India it symbolises purity and hence its use in wedding gowns. Red is linked to our basic survival mode and therefore has strong masculine energies associated with its use.

Fast food restaurants often use red in their décor as it stimulates the appetite and encourages diners to eat fast and then leave, allowing for another sitting. In business it can stimulate clients to purchase but is best used in moderation and works well with its complementary colour green and also blue. Using red will always promote a sense of passion for anything you do, whether you are wearing it or using it in business. It will also get you noticed and heard.

Ask yourself what you need to do today and what emotions you are feeling that can be aided by mindfully wearing this passionate, exciting colour. In this chapter you will learn all about how to get complimented in red, and what qualities it can bring to your life.

The benefits of wearing RED

Are you looking for a new challenge and want to feel energised to succeed?

In psychotherapy red has been used to boost moods for depression, and so if you use this mindfully it can encourage you to come out of yourself and face life with renewed optimism. It can also be a wonderful colour to help you come up with new ideas as it is creative and propels you into action. Red will inject you with some enthusiasm to get going on a new project and the courage to do so.

If you have been rejected either in a relationship or from a job then you may be feeling very lacking in self-confidence. Red will help you to gain some new interest in life and help to give you some well needed energy to get up and go again.

Do you want to make a good impression at a job interview or get promoted and show your drive and enthusiasm?

Mindfully choosing to wear red to an interview shows you are ambitious, enthusiastic, motivated and dynamic. It will give you the confidence and assertiveness to project yourself as someone who wants to be noticed and is driven to succeed. Whilst you would make a great team player you could also be relied upon to head up any new project given to you.

If you are looking to get promoted you will need to show qualities of determination and passion for your job so that your employer can see you are excited about what you are doing, with a will to succeed.

Wearing red at work projects an image of being practical and someone who likes to get things done quickly. It shows that you are motivated and can work hard to achieve results. You appear driven to achieve your goals, and with your likeable personality enjoy teamwork as well as being capable of leading.

If you are going back to work after a period of absence then wearing red will give you the confidence to feel you have lots to offer an employer. Having been out of a business environment for a while it is easy to suffer from low self-esteem and feel inadequate due to all the technological changes that could have taken place in your absence.

Whilst red can be a great choice of colour at work, a word of warning. Too much red can be seen as aggressive which is not how you want to appear either in an interview or once in a job. So my advice is not to wear a red suit in its entirety but one of the following:

- Red jacket combined with neutral (grey, beige, black) trousers or skirt
- Neutral jacket combined with a red skirt (or trousers if appropriate)
- Neutral jacket and bottoms combined with a red shirt
- Red dress with a neutral jacket
- Red underwear
- Red handbag
- Red shoes or belt
- Red incorporated into a scarf pattern
- Red coloured stones in a necklace

Are you searching for romance and going on a date or making new friends and want to feel vital and confident or are you attending an event and would like to radiate health and happiness?

Scientists have proved that women dress to reflect how their bodies function and choose to wear red and/or pink when they are at their most fertile or when they are looking for a partner. Apparently wearing red on an Internet dating site means you are more likely to get noticed and contacted by men than women wearing other colours. Men are more likely to find a woman attractive in red, to ask her out and happier to spend more money on her if she is wearing red! Thus proving that colour can affect behaviour even on a subconscious level.

For both men and women if you mindfully choose to wear red when you are with your partner or on a new date, it shows them that you are a fun person who can be impulsive in love, but value their relationships and family deeply. Too much red can be intimidating for the receiver so take care not to overdo it. For women, wearing a red dress is the best way to get noticed and is the most feminine article to wear if looking for romance. For men, choose to incorporate red in a shirt pattern, a jumper or a tie or a dark red jacket.

Mindfully choosing to wear red to a social event will ensure you get noticed for all the right reasons. Whilst so many people around you will choose to dress in safe black you will glow with health and happiness if you wear the right shade of red for your colouring and personality, because this colour up against the face will reflect a glowing and rosy complexion. So get visible wearing red and brighten up everyone else's day as well as your own!

Are you about to sit exams and need some empowerment to keep you motivated?

If you are studying for exams and feel the need for some energy and creativity then wear red; it will help you to get motivated and keep you awake for longer if you need some extra adrenaline at the end of a long day studying. If you are unable to wear red because you are in a uniform of some kind, simply choose to wear a red vest or underwear, as any colour you wear up against your skin, even not seen, will have the same powerful benefits as seeing it.

Are you recovering from an illness or feeling tired and in need of a physical boost?

If you are recovering from an illness or depression red is a wonderful tonic; as it releases the hormone adrenalin it will give you an energy boost all day long. It also raises blood pressure as it stimulates the nervous system and increases circulation and the heartbeat. Red also helps to heal wounds, and ward off colds and chills by warming up the body. It has been used medically to heal rheumatism and helps with anaemia. Also, if you are exercising wearing red will increase your physical activity. You can wear red socks, a scarf, gloves or red underwear to heat up your body if you feel tired or about to go down with a virus or cold.

DON'T wear this colour in abundance if you have asthma, high blood pressure, a fever or heart problems or are particularly stressed or anxious. Red will only increase the problems.

Do you want to slim without dieting?

If you are trying to lose weight mindfully choose to wear red as it increases the circulation and metabolism, and as this colour is absorbed through your skin, not only will it help you to get moving and exercise but it will also give you some confidence along the way. Also if you are on a diet then eat red foods in abundance, i.e. strawberries, cherries, raspberries, red onions, tomatoes, peppers and spices, as these will give you an energy boost.

Are you in need of a physical tonic during the menopause or during the ageing process?

With menopause and ageing often comes increased tiredness. So, to maximise your energy levels and act as a physical tonic wear red and eat red foods which are high in vitamin C. Many women find that it is the start of the menopause that really triggers signs of ageing. With decreased hormones in the body, your colouring starts to fade and often women can feel invisible. Red is a wonderfully empowering colour to wear at this time, as it will make you still feel passionate about life and your future. It also shows the world that you are still an attractive, feminine woman who demands attention!

When NOT to wear RED

Be mindful about wearing red if you are feeling particularly anxious, find it hard to relax, are angry or have high blood pressure. Also avoid it if you don't want to stand out in a crowd and get noticed. Be careful of certain shades of red if you have a constant high cheek colour that will only highlight this area.

If RED is your No 1 mindful colour choice what does it say about your personality?

If your wardrobe is full of red, and lacks other colours then you are naturally portraying an energetic and motivated personality. You really enjoy life and are determined to achieve your goals, putting lots of decisive action into play.

You can be creative with originality and flair and get things done with courage and drive. If you find yourself too immersed in red, it can tend to make you want things to happen too quickly and frustration sets in. You can get too competitive and impulsive so consider adding some other colours into your wardrobe to complement your wonderfully enthusiastic nature.

Why I love RED

I remember in my youth that my mum never wore make-up or smart clothes during the day but often used to wear red when she went out socialising with my father. She literally changed into this beautiful, glamorous woman, and having been generally unwell for large periods of her life she told me she wore red to give her the confidence and energy to go out and feel well enough to enjoy herself at social events. So by the time I was old enough to be mindful of my own wardrobe choices, I associated red with looking and feeling radiant and healthy.

I went through a period in my twenties when first working in London and wearing red and black all the time. I can see now that early in my career it gave me the dynamic combination of wanting to be taken seriously in business, and having the drive and outgoing personality to achieve success.

What colours to wear with RED?

There are certain colours that work better with red than others. Some clash with it, some tone it down and some allow it to shine:

- *GREEN* is red's complementary (opposite on the colour wheel) and is therefore very dynamic when used together with the added benefit of balancing the more fiery aspects of red. Combining these two colours means that you can allow yourself to be driven from your heart. Green also has the added benefit of bringing down a high red/pink cheek colour if you have a tendency to blushing, flushing or broken veins.

- *BLUE* cools red down and therefore stops red causing you to feel too dominant or aggressive. A red top with blue denim trousers/skirt is a great combination.

- *YELLOW* gives you the wisdom to project yourself with drive and passion and to think before you act, but it's best to only wear small accents of yellow with red as these colours together don't work well for many. Use the combination in a scarf or wear yellow underwear.

- *GREY* combines well with red at work. Grey is a neutral colour that signifies you can be detached, have good judgement and are professional whilst allowing red's enthusiasm to shine through.

- *BROWN* works with red only in a business environment if in shades of beige or camel. These are conservative colours and allow red to be dominant.

- *WHITE* and red are very dramatic. White shows that you are clear about who you are and will highlight the shade of red you are wearing making it radiant.

- *CREAM* and red are a softer dynamic.

- *BLACK* and red are very striking and can be worn in business or as a smart outfit. Black gives the impression of being in control whilst red shows you are driven. A dynamic combination indeed.

Different shades of RED and which ones suit YOU best

Once you have decided you feel like wearing red as one of your mindful colours, what shade do you choose for optimum well-being?! It is pointless to wear a red jacket because you feel emotionally in need of the qualities this colour brings only to discover certain shades wash you out and make you look tired with a blotchy complexion. This is counterproductive to looking and feeling your best and gaining the mood boosting benefits of red.

There are many words to describe the different varieties of red: scarlet, pillar-box, vermillion, burgundy, crimson, cardinal, strawberry, maroon and ruby, but which one will make you look radiant and healthy with a glowing complexion and sparkling eyes?!

A word of warning – if you are one of those women or men that blushes easily, has a high cheek colour or broken veins, please be careful when wearing red up against your face, it will only highlight this area on your skin and whilst some rosy colouring is healthy, any extra red against the face (particularly in bright cool shades) will just overemphasise it.

In the words of Christian Dior: "There is certainly a red for everyone." However, it is your individual colouring that will determine which shades of red suit you best. To keep things simple there are 4 categories that red falls into: blue-red and pure red for cool skin tones and bright red, and red-orange for warm skin tones.

1   Blue-red or raspberry pink will look flattering with your pink based skin tone and soft features for everyone with the summer colouring.

2   Pure red and burgundy are stunning on the cool dramatic

features and colouring of the winter season, enhancing definitions on the face.

3   Bright red on a yellow/golden spring skin tone is wonderfully striking, a colour some with warm skins love but shy away from, so wear in small quantities if you feel overwhelmed by it.

4   Red-orange is the best colour for more autumnal types with a bronze based skin tone, and looks glorious with brown eyes and dark or golden hair.

To discover which shades of RED suit YOU best, follow my draping method below. You will need:

- A mirror that is large enough to see yourself from the waist up.
- Lighting that is as bright and natural as possible. If you must be in artificial light then use fluorescent bulbs.
- To be against a background that is plain and colourless, preferably white.
- For women to remove all make-up. You need a clean and clear face.
- To be clear of all jewellery round your neck.
- To keep your glasses on if you wear them so you can see yourself clearly.
- Some different shades of red to test against your face.
- To drape the red shade on your shoulders making sure it reflects up against your skin.

What you WANT to see

1   An even skin tone
2   A reduction of skin blemishes and any high cheek colour/broken veins
3   Your skin looking clearer and fresher
4   Your eyes sparkling and the whites looking brighter
5   Your own natural colouring being enhanced

6   An absence of dark lines under the chin and shadows under the eyes

7   That the lines and wrinkles have been lifted

What you DON'T want to see

8   An emphasis on skin blemishes or red blotches

9   Any exaggeration of a high cheek colour

10   A patchy white complexion

11   An accentuation of lines and wrinkles

12   An accentuation of dark shadows under the eyes or chin

13   A tired, unhealthy appearance

14   Your lips looking darker (which may happen with very dark red)

Once you have done this test, you should now know which shades of red look fabulous on you and belong to your mindful colour palette, and which ones you need to avoid. If you really can't tell, ask someone you can trust to be honest with you. The most important thing is that the shade should make you smile when you see yourself in it. If wearing red is simply not appealing to you then why not find yourself some jewellery with red stones which will give you the same benefits, or wear some red underwear or some red accessories.

A case study – Jane

I have a friend I grew up with called Jane. From my earliest memory of her in the playground at school she always wore a red duffel coat. I badly wanted that coat as it looked warmer than all the others and she always got friends to play with her because she got noticed all the time.

When we ended up sharing a flat together after leaving school she had another red coat, this time a beautiful designer wool one that had gorgeous gold buttons that made it even more desirable. She loved it so much that twenty years later having worn it to pieces, she cut it up and used squares of it to make a patchwork cushion!

Jane has olive skin with green eyes and dark brown hair, and red is the colour that suits her best. Not only does it flatter her complexion and make her look youthful and healthy, but it is the colour that she feels gives her energy and confidence in everything she does.

Jane is a very creative person, and makes her own curtains and bedspreads. She often balances wearing red with green, its complementary best friend and her other favourite colour. She says, "I have always loved red and remember even as a small child demanding that my mother buy me a red coat! It has been the colour that makes me feel the most comfortable throughout my life; through all the highs and lows I always find myself choosing red and am sure I always will!"

Chapter 6

Mindfully *Pink – Choose your shade of pink and feel compassion and love*

Do you need help letting go of the past, releasing old habits and emotional conditioning?
Are you feeling lonely at the end of a relationship or embarking on a new romance?
Have you been sad or depressed and need to start loving yourself again?
Do you work in a caring profession and want to share your compassion?
Are you pregnant or a young mother and need some nurturing?
Do you want to feel feminine and youthful during the ageing process or the menopause?

Getting some pink into your life will help you emotionally, physically and psychologically by enhancing all of the above. Before delving into the benefits of wearing pink and what shades will suit you best for optimum well-being, let's have a look at the background to this beautiful, compassionate colour. It will help you to understand a bit about its power and why you may want to choose it as one of your mindful colours.

PINK Background

Pink has always been associated with feminism and still is. Think pink for the Breast Cancer Awareness Campaign, Barbie dolls and My Little Pony.

Although times are changing, most women will relate to being brought up in a world full of pink, fluffy comfort toys and dresses. It's no wonder that in our modern colour conditioning world, most children given choices will choose blue if they are a boy and pink a girl. However, it didn't always used to be this way. The pink is for girls, blue is for boys gender stereotype seems to be a marketing misconception. For hundreds of years before the 18th century babies were dressed in non-gendered colours, normally white.

Jo Paoletti writes in her book *Pink and Blue: Telling the Boys from the Girls in America*, "Our great-great-great grandparents and their ancestors were more concerned about distinguishing children and babies from adults than boys from girls. Pink and blue were suggested as interchangeable, gender-neutral nursery colour, appearing together in many of the clothes and furnishings found in the baby's room."

It wasn't until the end of the 19th century when famous psychologists claimed childhood theories that parents started to differentiate between the genders and the colour associations became more fixed. Blue was considered a more serious and studious colour therefore more appropriate for boys, and pink with softness and youth therefore more appropriate for girls.

As the feminist movement took hold in the late 20th century, pink became known as a girlie, childish colour, associated with all things glittery. However, it really came into fashion when pink ribbons became the symbol of Breast Cancer Awareness month, empowering pink as a survival colour and chosen apparently for its femininity. Ironic when you consider that in the 18th century pink ribbons were given to baby boys when they were born and young boys wore pink uniforms. In Belgium today baby boys are still dressed in pink – and why not?!

To highlight the use of pink as a feminist colour today, there is a 100,000 strong group of women in India called the Gulabi (pink) Gang. All of the women wear bright pink saris and wield bamboo sticks in pursuit of justice, as domestic and sexual violence are commonplace in their rural area. They have stood up for their rights amongst their families and villages, and are now bringing about system changes through direct action and confrontation. A powerful collaboration of pink!

In South Korea female-friendly pink parking spaces have been created at a massive expense which authorities say have been made for safety purposes. The "she spots" are longer and wider than average parking spaces and are marked with bright pink lines and a logo, intended for women only. The pink stereotype remains firmly in place in our modern world it would seem.

The colour pink itself derives its name from the flowers known as "pinks" in the 17th century. Magenta, however, is a shocking bright pink and only came about in the 20th century due to the evolvement of stronger colour dyes.

Pink also has beneficial properties psychologically. An article in the *International Business Times* in 2013 reported that prisons in Switzerland were using pink to calm down inmates by putting them in a pink painted cell. This project was called "Cool Down Pink" and they painted a total of 30 cells across various Swiss jails in this colour. Psychologist Daniela Spath said that because pink is known to have a calming and physically soothing effect they were applying this colour therapy principle in the project.

Ms Spath said that the level of anger can lessen in as fast as 15 minutes but the prisoners are usually confined within the pink cell for about 2 hours; but whilst the colour can affect moods in a positive way it didn't necessarily mean that all the prisoners were glad to be surrounded by pink walls as pink is often associated with 'being girly' thereby inferring that men are weak.

The report also stated that aside from the prisons, there were some police stations that had also used pink, reporting that the project seemed to work since most of those they arrested quietened down and even slept faster in the coloured pink room.

Pink is a combination of red and white and is therefore considered a 'tint' and not a pure primary colour. This is a gentler colour than red and is known more as a compassionate and loving colour than red's fiery passionate nature. It is a nourishing and supportive colour that symbolises unconditional love to the wearer, so if you are reading this chapter because you either consciously or subconsciously need the strength that this colour brings you there are many shades to choose from, depending on your mood and your needs and which ones suit your own personal colouring the best. When it comes to benefitting your health, strong bright fuchsia and magenta can increase your blood circulation, relieve headaches and tiredness.

The benefits of wearing PINK

Do you need to let go of the past, release old habits and emotional conditioning?

We all get trapped into old habits and past conditioning. Sometimes the hardest part is waking up to the realisation that you need to relinquish emotional patterns and move forward. If you have found yourself too dependent on others for support and love in the past and need to let go of any difficult or hurtful situations, pink is a nurturing colour that will allow you to feel unconditional love for yourself and to forgive others.

If you have unhappy memories and need to release events from the past then pink will help you to heal open wounds that have caused psychological turmoil. These could be anything from your upbringing, parents, schooling, marriage or job. Surrounding yourself in the loving colour of pink will help you to feel gratitude too.

Magenta is the best shade of pink to wear to harness the power of letting go. Anything that is holding you back can be helped to be released by selecting a hot pink shade which will enable you to move forward and accept the natural progression of your life.

What is really important is to believe in yourself and pink can help you to do this. Wearing pink will allow you to get in touch with your powerful and loving feminine persona, to feel more at ease within yourself and to be able to accept any love that comes your way!

If you have experienced the break-up of a relationship and are feeling sad, depressed or lonely then wearing pink will help to give you the strength to carry on and to value yourself. It might be a time when you need to learn to love who you are as perhaps you have given away too much of yourself to someone else. It could also be time to stop others from downloading all their issues on to you!

When you are ready to embrace a new relationship, either a romantic one or a new friendship or perhaps reconcile with a family member who you have had problems with in the past, pink will help you to let go, move on and show you are a compassionate person whilst loving yourself for your own special qualities. It will help you to feel centred in your own power.

Pink is a wonderful colour to choose to help create security and safety within an existing relationship too. If you can learn to love yourself, then think about it, you become more lovable to others too. So if you are embarking on a new romance, wear pink; it will endear you to a new partner, as you will be projecting yourself as someone who is loving and tender.

Men like seeing women in pink as apparently they find it sexy and feminine because subconsciously it is the closest thing to resembling flesh! No doubt this relates back to our ancestral heritage of how cavemen and women used to behave and dress. Men are also starting to wear a lot more pink particularly in the workplace where fashions are becoming more casual, and pink shirts and ties are now favoured in many corporate businesses.

Do you work in a caring profession and want to share your compassion?

Pink has to be worn carefully in a normal corporate environment and worn subtly as a shirt or top with a suit or smart jacket, or perhaps as an accent colour in a scarf. It can be perceived as being too feminine in some very traditional practices. However, where pink really does come into its own is if you work in one of the caring professions: as a nurse, counsellor, with children, social work or with sick or the elderly.

It is because of pink's nurturing and caring qualities that this is such a beautiful colour to wear with people in need of pink's healing energies. Anyone that you come into contact with when wearing pink will feel at ease immediately with you, and will be able to open up and share their problems with you. Magenta in particular is viewed as a highly spiritual colour that offers unconditional loving.

Do you need to nurture yourself and your child if you are pregnant or a young mother?

Pink is such a nurturing, compassionate colour and I remember being pregnant with my daughter and wearing an unusual amount of pink, as it's not one of my favourite colours. I was choosing pink subconsciously at the time, as it was only recently finding photographs of that time I realised in almost every one I was wearing an item of pink. It's not surprising as it is such a warm, gentle colour, and when you are pregnant the feelings of protection and nurturing can be incredibly strong. Of course when your baby is born you can experience mixed emotions of intense love but sometimes overwhelming responsibilities.

Choosing to mindfully pick pink can act as a muscle relaxant when you are stressed and tense, and pink relates to the reproductive organs so can help settle your hormones after giving birth. Babies male or female will all benefit from being wrapped in pink, loving clothing, so don't gender associate. All babies have spent months in a pink, nurturing womb so putting them in this colour when born will simply allow them to carry on feeling safe and protected in the wonderful energies that pink can bring them.

Do you want to feel feminine and youthful during the ageing process or the menopause?

There is no doubt ageing and menopause can leave you feeling less than feminine. Obviously this is not just psychological but a physical process too. The combination of diminishing hormone levels affecting your body and the realisation that you are no longer 'fertile' can make women feel vulnerable.

In a recent newspaper article entitled, "Women feel 'invisible' to men by the age of 51", health expert Eileen Durward from herbal remedies company A. Vogel says, "The world can feel very geared toward appreciating younger women, leaving those of a certain age to feel neglected or less worthy. These women are not invisible and neither are their concerns." If you haven't been particularly drawn to pink in the past, consider it now as a colour to wear. Whilst soft pastel pinks are seen as gentle and nurturing, the stronger brighter shades will help you to express your emotions and become more confident. Magenta is a vibrant and sensual colour that is youthful, so embrace it at this important time of change. It will also help to inject some excitement and fun into your life.

Pale PINK and MAGENTA – the difference!

I would just like to explain the different energies that pale and vibrant pink have. Whilst pale pink is healing and soothing it can be seen as a more submissive colour, and too much of it can be physically weakening. Surrounding yourself in too much pale pink can have a negative effect and cause a disinterest in life whilst stronger bright pinks and magenta will have a positive effect and encourage you to get on with things. Wearing all shades of pink indicate you are a warm, loving individual, but too much pale pink suggests you can be vulnerable, and willing to put others first whereas magenta is a more dynamic and self-confident colour. Combining the two or balancing with greens and blues is the best way to wear pale pink.

When NOT to wear PINK

Don't wear pink if you are feeling particularly emotionally vulnerable and find yourself giving more than receiving. If you are overly dependent on others avoid pink for the time being.

If PINK is your No 1 mindful colour choice what does it say about your personality?

If pink is your first colour choice, then you are a kind, generous person who loves to give and to nurture. You are loving and compassionate, and generally like to please others. You are feminine and romantic and enjoy being creative, especially with all things beautiful. If you find yourself wearing too much pink you may end up being too dependent on others, and feeling overly sensitive. Check out my list below on other colours that complement pink, and see if you can find one or two that will balance out your naturally compassionate nature.

What colours to wear with PINK?

There are certain colours that work better with pink than others. Some harmonise beautifully, whilst others look wonderfully dynamic:

- *BLUE* is very complementary with pink. Turquoise stands out with magenta and navy blue gives it a more 'grown-up' look.
- *GREEN* puts some strength and balance into pink, grounding it and giving it some depth. Bright green with rose pink is a beautiful combination.
- *ORANGE* clashes wonderfully with magenta and hot pink if you really want to get noticed.
- *WHITE* will reflect pink's femininity and delicateness, and offer freshness to it.
- *BLACK* really only works with icy cool pink and fuchsia which gives it a dynamic striking quality when worn by

anyone with cool colouring.

- *GREY* is a good 'neutral' colour to highlight pink and can be used in a business environment whilst keeping the look softer than black.

Different shades of PINK and which ones suit YOU best

Once you know that you need some pink in your life whether it's because you are feeling in need of support and love, or want to show others some tenderness, or feel like getting more into your feminine side, you will want to know which shades suit you best for optimum well-being and looking your best.

Pink ranges from the palest to hottest of shades: baby, shocking, pale, rose, orchid, Barbie, piggy, cherry blossom, carnation, salmon, magenta, fuchsia – to name but a few!

However, you need to understand which shades harmonise with the underlying base colour of your own complexion, otherwise pink could easily wash you out, and make your skin look blotchy and unhealthy. This is partly because pink is a mix of red and white. Therefore if you have a cool skin tone then most pinks will suit you and make you look healthy and pretty, but those with warm skin tones need to stick with the warmer shades of salmon and coral.

A word of warning – if you are one of those people that blushes easily, has a high cheek colour or broken veins, or even a haemangioma birthmark, please be careful when wearing pink up against your face; it can highlight your pink/red high colouring, and whilst some of your own natural pink colouring looks rosy and healthy any extra pink against the face (particularly in bright cool shades) will just overemphasise it.

Your colouring will determine which shades of pink suit you best. There are 4 categories that pink falls into: cool soft pastel pink, cool dynamic fuchsia pink, warm coral pink and warm peachy pink.

1   Cool pastel pink on a pink based skin will look lovely and flattering to the summer complexion, giving a rosy glow to the face.

2   Cool dynamic fuchsia pink is stunning on the very dramatic cool features and skin tone of the winter colouring.

3   Coral pink is very attractive on the warm yellow/golden skin tones of spring, the brighter the better.

4   Pink is not the best colour for bronze based autumn skin tones but the peachy salmon tones work well for you, with the more muted ones looking best.

To discover which shades of PINK suit YOU best follow my draping method below. You will need:

- A mirror that is large enough to see yourself from the waist up.
- Lighting that is as bright and natural as possible. If you must be in artificial light then use fluorescent bulbs.
- To stand against a background that is plain and colourless, preferably white.
- For women to remove all make-up. You need a clean and clear face.
- To be clear of all jewellery round your neck.
- To keep your glasses on if you wear them so you can see yourself clearly.
- Some different shades of pink to test up against your face.
- To drape the shade of pink over your shoulders making sure it reflects up against your skin.

What you WANT to see

1   An even skin tone

2   A reduction of skin blemishes and a high cheek colour/broken veins

3   Your skin looking clearer and fresher

4 Your eyes sparkling and the whites looking brighter

5 Your own natural colouring enhanced

6 An absence of dark lines under the chin and shadows under the eyes

7 That your lines and wrinkles have been lifted

What you DON'T want to see

8 An emphasis on skin blemishes and any red blotches

9 A patchy white complexion

10 Highlighting of a 'high cheek' colour or blushing

11 An accentuation of lines and wrinkles

12 A tired, unhealthy appearance

13 Your lips looking darker

Once you have performed this test, you should now know which shades of pink look fabulous on you and belong to your mindful colour palette, and which ones you need to avoid. If you really can't tell, ask someone you can trust to be honest with you. The most important thing is that the shade should make you smile when you see yourself. If wearing pink doesn't appeal to you then think about pink underwear – whilst it remains hidden you will get the same benefits because the energy of this colour will be absorbed directly through your skin. Otherwise consider rose quartz as a piece of jewellery instead, or use pink accessories in the form of a scarf, handbag, or even nail polish and lipstick will do the trick nicely for women, and for men consider a tie or a scarf or pink socks!

A case study – Millie

Millie is a beautiful St Lucian lady and she loves pink, and I really mean LOVES it! As a child she grew up one of seven siblings and the one thing she wanted more than anything was a pink dress but her parents were not well off and with so many children to feed, clothing was simply not a priority. When she got married she made sure her pink desires came true. Not only did she have pink flowers and a pink cake but all her bridesmaids and maid of honour were dressed in bright pink. In fact she would have painted the church pink if she could have done.

I wondered how pink made Millie feel. In her words: "I believe pink is one of the most beautiful colours. Wearing or seeing people in the colour pink makes me feel uplifted and when I wear it I have an inner glow and feel very attractive. It is such a vibrant colour and it makes me feel happy.

I used to wear a lot of black until I read Jules' book *How Not to Wear Black* and I realised I was wearing it like a uniform and it really made me look invisible with my colouring. So I took a long look at my wardrobe and knew it was time to get out of the black and add more of the pink! It's the bright, fuchsia pink that looks fabulous on my dark complexion and everyone always compliments me when I wear it and I feel like my whole body is smiling."

Chapter 7

Mindfully *Orange – Choose your shade of orange and feel confident and full of self-esteem*

Do you need to overcome adversity or recover from the shock of an emotional trauma?

Would you like to feel less shy or more sociable and attract a partner, or friends?

Are you looking to get started on a new project and become more independent?

Do you need to bring some optimism, joy and confidence into your life?

Would you like to energise your body and soothe any digestive problems?

Getting some orange into your life will help you emotionally, physically and psychologically by enhancing all of the above. Before delving into the benefits of wearing orange and what shades will suit you best for optimum well-being, let's just have a look at the background to this wonderfully dynamic colour. It will help you to understand a bit about its power and why you may want to choose it as one of your mindful colours.

ORANGE Background

Orange is friendly, optimistic and creative, and is on the warm colour spectrum being a mixture of red and yellow, sharing both the adventurous and dynamic qualities of red and the joyous, happy yellow rays.

Orange can be found in nature where we see its glorious tones in the warm setting sun, and particularly during autumn when the leaves turn a beautiful golden orange as this season represents a transition between the heat of the summer and the coldness of winter.

Tints of orange in either peach, terracotta or coral are good for hospitals, schools and factories because of the stimulating and warming effects of this colour. As it can focus the mind on physical comforts it has the ability to activate the appetite, therefore helping people feel positively and creatively about food. Orange is often used in restaurants, but is more warming than its neighbour red, and as a vital, stimulating colour encourages good conversation and happy dining.

Due to its uplifting qualities it is helpful for those suffering from depression or after an emotional shock or trauma. It will instil confidence, spontaneity and adventure in the wearer.

Before the 15th century orange didn't have a name and was simply called yellow-red. It wasn't until the late 15th to early 16th centuries that it got its name through orange trees brought to Europe from Asia by Spanish and Portuguese traders.

The Principality of Orange in Southern France housed the House of Orange-Nassau, one of the most influential royal houses in the 16th and 17th centuries. The colour became synonymous at that time with Protestantism, due to their religious connections and it was the Protestant William III who made orange a political colour in Europe. Orange is now the national colour of the Netherlands, because their royal family owns the Principality of Orange.

Orange became an important colour to all Impressionist painters, such as Monet, Renoir and Cézanne, which carried through into the Post-Impressionist era with bolder, more exper-imental uses of the colour, particularly enjoying combining it with its complementary colour blue to create drama and vivid backgrounds.

Orange is a colour of high visibility and is worn by rescue workers all over the world, particularly those at sea as life jackets are orange and lifeguards wear this colour. It is also a colour worn by workmen on motorways and cyclists on roads so as not to get hit by cars.

In religion orange has always been a highly revered colour. In both Hinduism and Buddhism it is the colour of the robes and indicates wisdom, and in Ancient China it was given the status as the highest colour of transformation.

In our modern world the colour orange is associated with joy, entertainment, fun and sociability, helping us to look on the bright side of things particularly in troubled times. In the words of the great late Frank Sinatra, "Orange is the happiest colour."

If you have trouble sleeping researchers are now proving that artificial light can block melatonin levels in the brain that help you to sleep naturally. These occur in so many of our modern day machines and light bulbs with the worst offender being blue light, which whilst beneficial during the day is not at night. They have found that one of the ways to counteract this effect is to wear orange or amber sunglasses. Orange is a warm, inviting colour and encourages extroversion and good communication. If you use it as a colour in the entrance of your home it will instantly make people feel welcome. However, some people find certain shades of orange overpowering, so if you are thinking of using it as a colour in your décor make sure everyone you live with shares your love of the chosen shade.

So is orange one of your mindful colours, and if so which shades suit you best? Also, think about what you need to do today and what emotions you are feeling that can be aided by wearing it. In this chapter you will learn all about how to get complimented in orange, and how its wonderful warming and heartening qualities can be brought into your life.

The benefits of wearing ORANGE

Do you need to overcome adversity or recover from the shock of an emotional trauma?

Orange has a positive effect and will help you to recover after a difficult period which has left you feeling deep grief or despair, and an inability to pick yourself up and feel positive about life. Wearing orange will allow you to feel secure and grounded enough in yourself to move out beyond your immediate surroundings and comfort to create new relationships and experiences.

If you have been through an emotional trauma, or shock of any kind, then orange really can help you move forward and leave the fear behind. This could be the break-up of a relationship, or anything that has affected you on a deep emotional level and left you feeling shocked or hurt.

Orange relates to your power centre which is the seat of your intuition, so listen to the emotional guidance that comes from your instincts, and not always from your head.

Your feelings are your only true reality, and if you have buried, unresolved traumas then wearing orange will help you to get in touch with them, bring them out into the open and start dealing with them by listening to your needs.

Would you like to be less shy or more sociable and attract a partner or friends?

Orange is the colour of confidence and sociability. It invokes good conversation, communication and interaction, and will have you thinking and talking all at once! If you wear this colour it will attract others to you, and allow you to feel at ease in company and in touch with your sexuality. If you feel lacking in self-worth and individuality leaving you shy in social environments, orange will give you the freedom to be yourself and to push your boundaries and meet new people.

Often conditioning as a child inhibits us, and if you relate to this then orange will allow your inner feelings to be expressed. Perhaps you are going through a period of tiredness or recuperation and are finding it increasingly difficult to get the energy to go out and socialise, or looking for a new partner and want to get some confidence to go out and meet new people? Orange is the colour of the risk taker but in a warm, vibrant way, so it will encourage you to come out of yourself, be playful and have some fun!

Are you looking to get started on a new project and become more independent?

If you find it difficult to get started on a project, be it spring cleaning your home, getting a new hobby or starting a new career, orange can really help you to get going. Change can be hard to embrace, but because orange is the colour of activity, adventure and high spirits these qualities will help you to go out there and explore, be creative and achieve those goals you have set yourself.

If you have been in a long relationship and or found yourself in a cycle of addictive behaviour, then orange can help you to break away, and become more independent. Orange will give you the energy to get up and go to leave behind all that you have known to be safe and familiar. So mindfully choose orange and get out of the rut of predictability and follow your gut instincts.

Do you need to bring some optimism, joy and confidence into your life?

If you have been feeling depressed or lacking in self-confidence then orange is the best colour to wear. As orange is a mixture of dynamic, driven red and more calming yellow it carries their qualities, but in a balanced combination of warmth, optimism and joy.

Wearing orange will make you feel brave and daring, bringing you some confidence to get out there and create some action. Presenting yourself as being active and fun loving will automatically make you feel happier and attract people to you who enjoy being in your company.

If you find wearing orange too stimulating or overpowering then wear it in small doses. An accent of orange, peach, coral or salmon in a scarf or a pattern in a shirt for instance will still give you all the wonderful benefits of orange and help you to feel more confident and happy.

Would you like to energise your body and soothe digestive problems?

Orange is a stimulating colour and therefore raises body heat and blood pressure, increasing circulation. As the colour of calcium it is fabulous for healthy nails, hair and bones, which is helpful if you are pregnant or know someone who is, and will encourage breast milk too.

This also means that if you are immobile in your hips or knee joints orange will encourage flow and movement. Orange is particularly beneficial for bringing balance to your digestive organs, in particular the stomach, spleen and pancreas. Where there is under-activity in this area, bloating or constipation wear orange on your bottom half or eat orange coloured foods. Orange is also a wonderful tonic for your liver and helps with a hangover and any form of alcohol overindulgence.

When NOT to wear ORANGE

Beware of using orange if you are overly stressed or easily angered and irritated, or have high blood pressure. If you feel particularly nauseous avoid orange.

If ORANGE is your No 1 mindful colour choice what does it say about your personality?

If you love to wear orange and it's your first choice out of the wardrobe then this represents someone who is warm-hearted, energetic and full of vitality.

You are optimistic and motivated which makes you someone other people love to have around, as you are sociable and enjoy conversing. Your natural outgoing nature is infectious and you probably have many friends. With your empathetic and warm personality people are easily drawn to you. Beware of overdosing on orange and not balancing it with other colours. This can make you slightly extreme and overactive!!

Why ORANGE is my favourite mindful colour!

When you get a positive reaction to a colour you are wearing, naturally it makes you want to wear it regularly. I have to stop myself wearing too much orange because I know that I can overdo it and then feel overly stimulated. However, orange is a colour that I love and I do believe loves me back!

When I wear it, in most shades other than very light or very dark, I get complimented or told how well I look; it's my chosen mindful colour when I need to feel confident and self-assured. Orange makes me feel uplifted and positive. It makes me smile and I feel happy within myself. It's a colour I choose to wear a lot socially because it fills me with confidence as well as warming up my complexion. I also love to wear amber stones set in gold which look gorgeous as a necklace and ensure that I get some of orange's wonderful qualities if I am not wearing it in my outfit.

What colours to wear with ORANGE?

There are certain colours that work better with orange than others. Some clash with it, some balance it and others sing along with it:

- *BLUE* is the complementary colour (the opposite on the colour wheel) to orange and is therefore balancing and brings some calmness to orange's stimulating energies.

- **BROWN** is very grounding and adds stability and a sense of security when worn with orange. Wear shades of brown to suit you, together with orange to create a rich warm wardrobe palette.
- **GOLD** and orange together are truly stunning! The warmth and harmony of these two colours together is glorious and they bring out the best of each other.
- **FUCHSIA** and orange clash and will get you some undivided attention! These two colours can be worn together but in small amounts in a pattern and not in large amounts of block colours unless you are brave enough to carry this off. Together they signify what fun you are.
- **WHITE** and **CREAM** are summery and highlight the natural light energies of orange's positivity and ability to communicate with an open mind. A refreshing and simplistic look.
- **GREY** and orange work very well together as a professional pairing. Grey brings detachment and competence and a maturity to orange's natural sunny and warm personality.
- **BLACK** and orange are a striking combination of warmth and coolness. Wearing black which is mysterious and protective will tone down orange's outgoing nature, so balancing the introvert and extrovert and giving you a powerful presence.

Different shades of ORANGE and which ones suit YOU best

Once you have decided you want to wear orange, which shade do you choose for optimum well-being? The darker shades whilst looking rich and vibrant on some of you with dark skins will often wash out those of you with pale skin tones. For many people, paler shades of peach, apricot, coral and salmon will be more flattering. For women peach rather than pink make-up is wonderful for alleviating a high cheek colour, due to flushing, blushing or broken veins.

The orange tones are often associated with the season of autumn, with the rich colours of russet and terracotta giving a warm glow to the countryside. These shades suit very warm and dark complexions and look glorious mixed with other colours of the autumn scene, like olive green, chocolate brown and gold.

If you find yourself struggling to wear orange then buy some orange coloured gemstones as these have wonderful orange properties of their own so will do the job beautifully. Otherwise consider buying a top in orange or a scarf, or for men a tie. Choose a budget item that allows you to wear it in small doses to see how you feel about it and gauge others' reactions. If all goes well, you can splash out on your chosen shade of orange in the future.

Your colouring will determine which shades of orange suit you best. To keep things simple there are 4 categories that orange falls into: cool pastel peach, cool dark salmon pink, warm bright orange and warm burnt orange.

1   Cool pastel peach is the lightest version of orange and pretty on a very cool summer pale complexion but best to ensure the shade is closer to pink than orange.

2   Cool dark salmon pink is the preferred shade of orange on a very cool winter skin tone. Again the emphasis on the pink rather than orange suits this complexion best.

3   Warm bright orange is a gorgeous colour on yellow based spring complexions along with peach and coral.

4   Warm burnt orange looks rich and glamorous on a darker skinned or bronze based autumn complexion.

To discover which shades of ORANGE suit you best, follow my draping method below. You will need:

- A mirror that is large enough to see yourself from the waist

up.
- Lighting that is as bright and natural as possible. If you must be in artificial light then use fluorescent bulbs.
- To stand against a background that is plain and colourless, preferably white.
- For women to remove all make-up. You need a clean and clear face.
- Be clear of all jewellery round your neck.
- To keep your glasses on if you wear them so you can see yourself clearly.
- Some different shades of orange to test against your face.
- To drape the shade of orange over your shoulders making sure it reflects up against your skin.

What you WANT to see

1 An even skin tone
2 A reduction of skin blemishes
3 Your skin looking clearer and fresher
4 Your eyes sparkling and the whites looking brighter
5 Your own natural colouring enhanced
6 An absence of dark lines under the chin and shadows under the eyes
7 That the lines and wrinkles have been lifted

What you DON'T want to see

8 An emphasis on skin blemishes
9 A patchy white complexion
10 Any red blotches or an orange tinge to your skin
11 An accentuation of lines and wrinkles
12 An accentuation of dark shadows under the eyes or chin
13 A tired, unhealthy or dull appearance

Once you have done the above test, you should know which shades of orange look fabulous on you and belong to your mindful colour palette and which ones you need to avoid. If you really can't tell, ask someone you can trust to be honest with you.

The most important thing is that the shade should make you smile when you see yourself in it. If you really don't like being seen in it then consider wearing orange or peach underwear against your skin which will allow the qualities of this warming colour to be absorbed into your system.

A case study – Helen

Helen Kendall-Tobias is a colour consultant and a personal stylist, and her favourite colour is coral – a beautiful shade of orange. This is how she came to love it: "In recent years I have had a real love of bright colours – think picnic baskets with bright blues, lime greens, hot pinks and particularly citrus orange. So it's hard to explain what drew me to this coral colour – as it's really out of character.

I've never been one for romantic, pretty styles and my clothing personality has been fairly classic, albeit with a twist. I was walking through House of Fraser at Bluewater one day and in need of something to keep me warm during cooler summer evenings.

I came across a fine knitted sweater with broad white and coral bands and next to it was the scarf to match, a plain cotton linen pashmina-style shawl. In truth there were two scarves next to each other – one was golden beige and the other coral.

At the time I bought both as I wasn't sure about the coral – but once home and trying things on again, I realised it was the coral I loved (so I returned the golden beige scarf).

As a personal stylist, I spend much of my working life helping ladies to plan and organise their wardrobes. So I think my love of strong colours serves to complement my attitude to work, and as a self-employed person my need to get things done quickly and off my to-do list.

When I put this outfit combination on, and particularly the

scarf, I'm really in personal time – as it's not something I would wear with clients. When I wear coral I feel able to let the world float on by, without the need to get involved. I don't feel like charging around and getting things done and I feel much more confident of my own needs. Also I do feel more 'girly' in this colour because it probably brings out a softer side to my personality.

I think it goes with my red-orange hair quite well, again a colour that I turned to only recently having been blonde for umpteen years..."

Chapter 8

Mindfully *Yellow – Choose your shade of yellow and feel joyful and happy*

Do you need to make decisions and find clarity of mind?
Are you feeling depressed or unhappy and need to brighten up your life?
Are you fearful and would like to feel full of joy and hope?
Do you need detachment to gain a clearer view of a situation?
Are you studying for an exam and need to still your mind for maximum concentration?
Do you need to instil some inspiration and creativity into your working life?

Getting some yellow into your life will help you emotionally, physically and psychologically by enhancing all of the above. Before delving into the benefits of wearing yellow and what shades will suit you best for optimum well-being, let's just have a look at the background to this joyous colour. It will help you to understand a bit about its power and why you may want to choose it as one of your mindful colours.

YELLOW Background

Yellow is a warm spectrum colour and the lightest, with its wavelength lying between orange and green. This is the colour that resembles the sun and therefore makes us feel warm and happy with its aura of brightness and joy. Wearing yellow indicates you are full of self-confidence, are a great communicator and that you enjoy life.

Your positive and optimistic nature is welcomed by others making you popular and well liked. As yellow is the colour of the intellect it aids all creative pursuits and helps with feelings of depression, fear and unhappiness.

Yellow is a colour that encourages hope and optimism helping you to feel happy and relaxed. It is also associated with wisdom and intelligence. Yellow has a positive physical effect on your nervous system and muscles, and can help assist the function of the liver, encouraging digestive juices. This colour's most powerful properties can assist with all inflammatory conditions, such as arthritis and rheumatism.

In ancient times yellow and gold were considered divine symbols of creation, with gold in particular being revered as symbolising the sun. Yellow was associated with love in the early Greek and Roman times, but gradually yellow lost its favour and became associated with promiscuity and treachery, particularly associated to Judas Iscariot in Christian times. This bad image lasted up until the 20th century. Even now in our culture we signify the end of a love affair with yellow roses so yellow also became a colour of jealousy and betrayal.

In religious symbolism, Christianity in the Middle Ages associated yellow with gold, in Hinduism it was worn by holy men, and the Buddhists wear saffron robes as a sign of their commitment to the order.

Yellow was one of the first colours used in prehistoric cave art. The 19th century painter JMW Turner was one of the first famous artists to use yellow in his work to signify emotions. Vincent Van Gogh loved using yellow to depict sunlight, and we all know one of his most famous paintings produced in 1888, *Sunflowers*, and his stunning use of different shades of yellow.

In the 20th century yellow became popular due to its visibility, which remains today as seen in our rescue vehicles, football penalty cards, taxis in New York, and school buses in Canada.

We associate yellow colours mainly with flowers: daffodils, primroses, marigolds, buttercups, sunflowers and also with lemons, butter, canaries and saffron. The complementary (opposite on the colour wheel) colour to yellow is violet, and these colours can be used together in the clothes you wear or colours in your home, to create maximum contrast and harmony.

In my experience yellow is the colour that women in particular have the most problem wearing. They often recognise how much it suits me (because I work in yellow a lot) but comment on how they look dreadful in it! I have to educate women on how fabulous anyone can look in yellow, because believe me it's all down to the chosen shade. I went on a mission a while ago and visited the Great British High Street. I asked women whether they were tempted to buy something yellow – almost all of them said they really wanted to but were scared it didn't suit them. Only one lady said she had a yellow top in her wardrobe but had never worn it!

Yellow is also associated with self-love. When I tell women this they often sigh and recognise that perhaps that could be the subconscious reason they have a problem with it. How many women including yourself do you know that really love themselves? Women spend most of their lives making a living out of loving others and often forget about nurturing themselves. Yellow therefore is a very important emotional colour for women. Men, however, can also really benefit from wearing small amounts of yellow as tints in their work shirts or as ties, which can look really fabulous teamed with a navy or dark grey suit.

So is yellow one of your chosen mindful colours and if so which shades suit you best? Also, think about what you need to do today and what emotions you are feeling that can be highlighted by wearing it? In this chapter you will learn all about how to shine in yellow, and what joyous qualities it can bring to your life.

The benefits of wearing YELLOW

For decision making, emotional detachment and clarity of mind

Yellow is the colour of detachment so if you need to make an important decision it is a powerful tool in being able to step away from the situation and see it with clarity before you make your choices. If you find it difficult to make a decision due to self-doubt then yellow will help to give you the confidence you need to value yourself. As yellow is also the colour of the intellect it will enable you to stimulate and speed up your thinking processes and, in overcoming indecision, will allow you to trust in your gut instincts.

If you need to let go of a past situation or detach yourself from old habits then yellow is a great colour to embrace.

For overcoming fear, depression or unhappiness

Yellow is the colour of sunlight and joy, so if you are experiencing a period of unhappiness or depression in your life, just seeing this colour can be beneficial, so wearing yellow or placing it in your living environment is very powerful. Its cheerful, uplifting qualities are warming like the sun, and yellow helps you to get in touch with your special individual abilities, so gaining some self-belief can help you start to feel happy again.

When you feel out of balance in your life yellow can make you feel more in control and centred. Combine it with anything blue or violet, which are calming colours and together with yellow help with anxiety and stress, or if you are feeling particularly fearful about a situation. Yellow has the ability to fill you with hope that everything in your life will be alright, and to allow yourself to move forward in a positive and optimistic way.

For inspiration in your working life

Wearing yellow at work will not only make others smile when

they see you in such a sunny colour, but it will help you to feel more positive, creative and self-assured. When you feel in balance this colour will encourage you to take up new challenges, it stimulates your brain to allow for quick thinking and also allows your creative side to develop.

Wearing too much yellow at work can lead to overanxiety and an inability to relax so in order to keep the balance here is my advice on how to wear it:

- Wear a yellow shirt or jacket combined with neutral tones of grey.
- A navy blue jacket combined with a yellow top looks professional, and wear yellow up against your face to look healthy and attractive.
- Black or preferably a grey jacket with a yellow dress or patterned skirt looks smart.
- White or cream mixes well with yellow in warmer weather.
- Yellow underwear will give you all this colour's properties without being seen.
- A yellow handbag is a fabulous accessory in the spring and summer months.
- Yellow shoes are daring but will give a block colour outfit a flash of brightness.
- Gold jewellery is flattering up against the face for warm skin tones.
- Yellow in a patterned scarf will lift the complexion and is a wonderful accessory.

For studying and taking exams

If you or your children have exams or are studying then yellow is a brilliant colour for helping to still the mind, encourage creativity and concentration. Yellow can also help with decisiveness, acquiring knowledge, mental learning, clarity of thought, and quick thinking. If it isn't possible to wear yellow during an exam, make sure you get some yellow underwear; this is really effective as its qualities will be absorbed through your skin.

For healing inflammation and digestive problems

Yellow helps to support your nervous system and your muscles too, thereby increasing circulation. It is also a fabulous colour to aid the digestive system namely your gastric juices in the stomach, liver, gall bladder and pancreas. Aside from wearing yellow you can use lemons and grapefruits as internal cleansing fruits and applying calendula will help to heal problem skin conditions such as eczema and scar tissue.

Yellow has the ability to loosen any calcium deposits you may have built up over time in your system and so can aid all inflammatory conditions like rheumatism, arthritis and stiffness of the joints, and back problems.

When NOT to wear YELLOW

DON'T wear yellow in abundance if you are suffering from any mental or personality disorder or you are unusually overanxious or argumentative as this colour will be too mentally stimulating for you.

If YELLOW is your No 1 mindful colour choice what does it say about your personality?

If you opt to wear yellow at the slightest excuse then you are naturally sunny and optimistic. You are quick thinking and creative, original and inventive. You are curious and can be critical but that's because your mind enjoys the challenge of understanding things. Loving yellow above all others means that you like to push boundaries.

Beware of indulging in yellow though as too much of this glorious colour can make you egotistical and overly critical of others, with an inability to unwind and relax. Find other colours

I have suggested to ensure you keep a balance to your joyous outlook on life.

Why I love to wear YELLOW in the spring

The moment I see that first daffodil, I feel uplifted and happy knowing that spring and sunshine are just around the corner. After a long, cold winter there is nothing I like more than to put a vase of beautiful golden daffodils in my living room to brighten up my day and fill me with joyous hope of the season to come.

I have to admit to being a bit of a yellow groupie. Whenever I wear the warm golden shades I also get admired. Women often stop me and say how fabulous it looks and how they wish they could wear it! Sadly, it's a colour most women shy away from and I make it one of my main colour missions to get women loving this colour like I do.

The truth is that if you have a warm, yellow/golden or bronze based complexion you can wear it in abundance. If, however, you have a cool pink based skin tone, then yellow is not going to be your best colour and you will need to wear a cool shade or indulge in some yellow accessories instead.

I often wear yellow when I am doing talks or presentations as it is the colour of creativity and therefore helps me to communicate about colour in a passionate and intelligent way. I always combine yellow with either grey or blue in order to keep this glorious colour balanced.

Yellow is one of my mindful colour choices because it makes me feel happy, brings a smile to my face and to all those who see me in it – so how can I not love the visibility yellow gives me? Please try wearing yellow too – it really can be a wonderful tonic!

What colours to wear with YELLOW?

There are certain colours that work better with yellow than others. Some clash with it, some tone it down and some allow it to shine:

- **PURPLE** is the complementary (opposite on the colour wheel) to yellow and is therefore very dynamic when used together, and also benefits you by balancing the potentially overstimulating qualities of yellow with the calming aspects of violet.

- **BLUE** being such a popular colour is easier to wear than violet yet has the same calming properties. Yellow shades look professional with navy blue for work, and can be teamed with dark denim for a smart outfit or paler shades for a softer look.

- **GREY** combines really well with yellow at work. Grey is a neutral colour that signifies you can be detached and have good judgement, and are professional, a great combination with the sunny, positive appearance of yellow.

- **BROWN** will ground bright yellow, and any golden yellow with dark earthy browns will look rich and glorious.

- **WHITE** and **CREAM** are great for wearing with yellow in the warmer months. These neutral shades allow yellow to shine and also show a professionalism and clarity at work.

- **BLACK** and yellow whilst very striking need to be worn with care! I believe black should be worn with only small accents of yellow to make sure you don't end up looking like a bee!! Black shows you are in control whilst yellow's fun loving spirit is able to balance the black's serious aspects.

Different shades of YELLOW and which ones suit YOU best

Once you have decided you want to wear yellow what shade do you choose? I know from experience that most women are scared of yellow, so it's really important to experiment with different shades, to see which one makes your skin glow and hair look fabulous too.

If you have yellow undertones in your skin then you will be

able to wear pure yellow. If you have a more bronze based complexion then the golden tones will suit you better. If you have a cool skin tone then you need to keep your shades pastel pale or neon bright, without any hint of warmth. Most women when put in a shade of yellow that suits them find it so uplifting and are really excited to see how flattering it looks against their complexions, making it appear healthy and glowing. This is what wearing yellow will do for an underlying yellow or golden skin tone in particular.

If the strong yellow shades frighten you, and you have never worn them before buy something inexpensive like a top or T-shirt, that won't break the bank, and see how many compliments you get.

If you like the colour you can start to incorporate it into your wardrobe and perhaps splash out a bit more next time. If you don't want to wear a strong shade of yellow simply choose a cream based one; it will still benefit your complexion and emotionally give you the qualities yellow brings.

If wearing yellow is just not for you, then why not consider some yellow stones such as citrine with gold jewellery as it will have the same benefits. Also think about yellow accessories such as scarves, handbags and shoes, or ties for men. Wearing yellow underwear against your skin will allow the qualities of this special colour to be absorbed into your system.

Your individual colouring will determine which shades of yellow suit you best. To keep things simple there are 4 categories that yellow falls into: cool pastel yellow, cool neon yellow, warm bright yellow and yellow-gold.

1   Cool pastel yellow is light and summery on the soft, delicate summer colouring.
2   Neon yellow looks fabulous on the strong cool colouring of winter complexions.
3   Bright yellow and primrose shades look gorgeous on

yellow/golden spring complexions.

4   Yellow-gold and all the golden tones will bring out the autumn bronze based complexion beautifully, and looks glorious with golden hair, and blue or brown eyes.

To discover which shades of YELLOW suit YOU best, follow my draping method below. You will need:

- A mirror that is large enough to see yourself from the waist up.
- Lighting that is as bright and natural as possible. If you must be in artificial light then use fluorescent bulbs.
- To stand against a background that is plain and colourless, preferably white.
- For women to remove all make-up. You need a clean and clear face.
- Be clear of all jewellery round your neck.
- To keep your glasses on if you wear them so you can see yourself clearly.
- Some different shades of yellow to test against your face.
- To drape the shade of yellow over your shoulders making sure it reflects up against your skin.

What you WANT to see

1   An even skin tone
2   A reduction of skin blemishes
3   Your skin looking clearer and fresher
4   Your eyes sparkling and the whites looking brighter
5   Your own natural colouring enhanced
6   An absence of dark lines under the chin and shadows under the eyes
7   That the lines and wrinkles have been lifted

What you DON'T want to see

8   An emphasis on skin blemishes

9   A patchy white complexion
10 A sallow, dull looking complexion
11 A slight yellow colouring on your complexion
12 Any red blotches
13 An accentuation of lines and wrinkles
14 A tired, unhealthy appearance

Once you have done the above test, you should know which shades of yellow look fabulous on you and belong to your mindful colour palette, and which ones you need to avoid. If you really can't tell, ask someone you can trust to be honest with you. The most important thing is that the shade should make you smile when you see yourself in it.

A case study – Judith

Judith is now in her 70s and still a beautiful woman. She has been through a lot of difficulties in her life, cancer twice and a divorce in her 60s. Unlike so many women I come across, she loves to wear yellow. She says: "Yellow is a colour I know that many women find difficult to wear but it is now a colour that really appeals to me even though in the past I might have struggled to wear it. It's such a joyous colour and it always makes me smile. I only really like the primrose shade as anything stronger is too much for my colouring now that it has faded. I often get complimented when I wear yellow and particularly like to put on a yellow shirt or jumper when I go to my painting class as it helps me get more in touch with my creative side."

Chapter 9

Mindfully *Green – Choose your shade of green and feel contented and balanced*

Do you need to learn forgiveness to enable you to move forward?
Do you need to resolve trust issues within your relationships?
Do you need to let go of anger and/or grief in order to feel balanced?
Are you unusually stressed and anxious and need to calm down?
Do you need a new sense of motivation and direction in your life?
Does your body feel run-down and need a tonic or a hangover cure?

Getting some green into your life will help you emotionally, physically and psychologically by enhancing all of the above. Before delving into the benefits of wearing green and what shades will suit you best for optimum well-being, let's have a look at the background to this beautifully balancing colour. It will help you to understand a bit about its power and why you may want to choose it as one of your mindful colours.

GREEN Background

At the centre of the rainbow stands green. It is neither a warm nor cool colour so represents balance in all its glorious and natural form. A combination of yellow and blue, green is the colour of nature and we associate it with growth and new beginnings, from the first green shoots of spring that bring with them hope and optimism that uplift our spirits and bring harmony into our lives.

Our eyes need no adjustment to see green and therefore it is a restful colour to view. Therefore green provides a wonderful environment for decision making and instilling balance in all things.

In the Middle Ages when colour represented status, where red was worn by nobility, green was donned by merchants and the gentry. In ancient Egypt green was associated with good health, and the Romans saw it as the colour of Venus, who was the goddess of gardens. In the 18th and 19th centuries green was linked to the Romantic Movement in art and literature, and as clothing dyes became more sophisticated different shades of green became available in cloth to wear.

In our modern day world, we have the political Green Party, and Greenpeace and a green cross draws our attention to pharmacies all over Europe. Hospitals also paint their walls green and doctors often wear green gowns: this is to bring balance and healing into a sick environment and to relax patients. Green is not only associated with nature and all things new but also youth and innocence. A colour of neutrality in between the heat of red and the coolness of blue, green is centred and balanced and is also the colour of permission, with green traffic lights signalling a move forward and in America to gain a Green Card is to get accepted for residence.

The negative aspects of green relate to jealousy and envy, and poison too. This dates back to the 19th century when certain paints and dyes did indeed contain a highly toxic green chemical. We also have connotations of looking green when feeling sick, and in certain cultures it is seen as an unlucky colour.

In metaphysics, green is the colour of 'creative intelligence' and in Hinduism it represents the fourth chakra of the heart; and being a combination of optimistic yellow and calming blue, green inspires hope and security.

Green is the colour of fairness; able to see both sides to a problem, it can help in all decision making. It gives us strength and courage and a need to belong. Wearing green clothing particularly suits redheads or brunettes with chestnut accents. This is because green and red are complementary colours and automatically look stunning when combined.

So is green one of your mindful colour choices, and if so which shades suit you best? Also, think about what you need to do today, and what emotions are you feeling that can be aided by wearing it? In this chapter you will learn all about how to get complimented in green, and what qualities it can bring to your life.

The benefits of wearing GREEN

Do you need to forgive someone to enable you to move forward?

Wearing green will help you to forgive, and the relief can be incredibly profound. You can move forward in a positive way allowing space for renewal and growth. It is very difficult to embark on a new relationship if you still harbour feelings of resentment towards someone, but when you can forgive them, you are doing yourself a favour as the love can then be allowed to flow once more. Perhaps you actually need to forgive yourself in order for your own personal transformation to take place. In which case wear some green and mix it with pink, the colour of love and compassion.

Green is the colour of loyalty and faithfulness, and whilst not a passionate colour it enables a sense of peace and balance in relationships.

Do you need to resolve trust issues within your relationships?

Wearing green will enable you to see situations from all different angles with clarity and understanding. If you find yourself having trust issues within your relationships then this is a great colour to allow your partner some space and freedom because ultimately you will be able to trust your own deepest feelings of acceptance. Green is the great peacemaker and enables you to put yourself in someone else's shoes so you can experience their issues. This will open up your heart so you can see things clearly, and allows fair judgement.

If you can open up to follow your own truths then trust becomes less of a problem. Green is the colour of balance and if you can get centred in yourself then you can be more objective and trusting, giving yourself the space needed to create some distance from the problem facing you. Green also sets boundaries with relationships.

Do you need to let go of anger and/or grief in order to feel balanced?

We all go through periods of anger and grief; so many things in life can cause us to feel these negative emotions and they can be hard to shift at the best of times. Green, however, can be a real blessing. As the colour of physical and emotional balance, it can help to heal a broken heart and release any supressed emotions you may be harbouring of anger and grief.

Wearing green will help you to get in touch with your feelings and let them go. Your heart will be more balanced and you can grow in compassion and unconditional love – not an easy challenge for any of us!

When you are pushed to deal with lessons of the heart you are being tested to dig deep and let go of any unwanted emotions that can be damaging and depleting. Green is the colour of choice for getting in touch with your feelings, and seeing the world with love, so embrace it with all your heart and see how much better you feel.

Do you need a new sense of motivation and direction in your life?

If you are struggling to gain a sense of motivation or get some direction in your life then wearing green will help encourage you to take action particularly when you need to gain a different perspective on your life. Green aids in all decision making and change, so if you are stuck in a rut and can't see the wood for the trees, this is the colour to help move you into new possibilities.

Green will enable you to feel secure and balanced enough to take a risk and let go of old patterns and embrace new challenges. You can allow yourself to act from the heart and this is a powerful acknowledgement of acceptance. Combining the warm sociable shades of orange with green will energise you and give you the necessary push to act on your decisions.

Does your body feel run-down and need a tonic? Are you unusually stressed and anxious or do you have a hangover?!

If you are going through a particularly stressful or anxious period in your life then wearing some green will help to heal and balance your body. Green is beneficial for your sympathetic nervous system and can positively influence the whole of the chest area, including the heart and lungs.

If you are tired, prone to chest infections or heart problems then wear green as a top, shirt, jacket or jumper so that it covers this area of your body. Green is also a great colour to wear if you have a hangover as it calms the nervous system, and combined with blue and white will physically help to purify your system after a big night out. As green also helps to detoxify the liver it is a good tonic and acts as a mild astringent.

When NOT to wear GREEN

Beware wearing too much green at one time as it is naturally calming and therefore an overindulgence in this colour can sometimes bring on a period of inactivity. If you are experiencing feelings of jealousy or envy decrease its use in your clothing. Like the colour itself, create balance with the amount of green you wear and combine it with other colours.

If GREEN is your No 1 mindful colour choice what does it say about your personality?

If you reach for green every morning, then you are showing all those lovely qualities of friendliness and generosity of spirit. You are warm-hearted and strive for peace and balance in every area of your life, particularly in your relationships and all things emotional. You have an open and honest approach with others and expect the same in return.

You enjoy healthy debate and listen to all sides of an argument, always sticking to your own truth. If, however, you find yourself becoming overly jealous or insecure you may want to consider adding another colour to your outfits which will allow the balanced side of your personality to naturally dominate.

Why I mindfully choose GREEN

A few years ago I appeared on a television breakfast show, primarily discussing colours for the Queen's Jubilee. I then went into a London department store and dressed a couple of women who were shopping for an outfit. I had some great feedback from the show and an extraordinary number of women wanting to know where I had bought my green jacket from!

I had chosen to wear this particular colour because I knew I would be dealing with the general public and trying to persuade them to be filmed with me, which was a challenge in itself. I therefore needed good judgement to choose the right women, and to trust my innermost feelings when on spec I had to find the colour to suit their particular needs. Green kept me balanced and allowed me to make quick decisions which meant a great result for everyone concerned.

What colours to wear with GREEN?

There are certain colours that work better with green than others. Some look striking and others harmonious:

- **RED** is the complementary colour (opposite on the colour wheel) to green and is therefore very striking when combined. Red will fire up a passive green and give you drive and energy to make decisions from the heart when worn together.

- Bright **PINK** and lime green colours look shockingly fabulous together. Lime green is the colour of prosperity and pink is feminine and fun loving, a great combination best kept for leisure not business unless you work in a fashion/creative field.

- **BLUE** and green as a mix of colours are harmonious and will instil a feeling of peacefulness and calm reminding you of the benefits of being outdoors in nature.

- **ORANGE** as a warm and sociable colour will help you to reach outwards, and worn together with green will allow you to make clear decisions and take action.

- **GREY** looks sophisticated with all shades of green. These colours match well having similar qualities of detachment and fair judgement. You will achieve things in a quiet and professional way.

- **BLACK** with green looks smart and businesslike for work and also glamorous in the evening. Very dark shades of green may have black in them so beware of wearing up against the face if you have a warm skin tone.

- **BROWN** in dark rich shades of chocolate and chestnut go beautifully with the autumnal colours of olive green. The combination is earthy and grounding. Lime green looks striking with dark brown and is more playful than olive.

- **WHITE** and **CREAM** look fresh and summery with the lighter spring greens, and will lift the emotions and the spirits, also providing a fresh work look.

Different shades of GREEN and which ones suit YOU best

Once you have decided you feel like wearing green, which shade do you choose for optimum well-being?! It is pointless wearing a green coat because you feel in need of some balance in your life and as a physical pick-you-up if the chosen shade makes you look washed out and exhausted. This is obviously counterproductive to looking and feeling your best.

There are many words to describe the different varieties of green: olive, bottle, spring, mint, emerald, jade, lime, hunter, jungle, apple, fern, to name a few, but which ones will make you look radiant and healthy with a glowing complexion and sparkling eyes?

Your colouring will determine which shades of green suit you best. To keep things simple there are 4 categories that green falls into: cool pastel mint green, very dark cool green, warm bright spring green and warm olive green.

1   Pastel mint green is a soft, pretty colour and looks lovely on cool pink based summer skin tones with pale hair colour.

2   Very dark green whilst looking fabulous with dark hair and on very cool winter complexions may well age you so wear it away from your face.

3   Bright spring green and lime only truly look good on a warm, yellow based spring complexion and even though you may find these shades rather shocking to begin with, wear them in small amounts against your face and reap the rewards with compliments!

4   Olive green only looks really gorgeous on a warm, bronze based complexion. As an autumnal colour it flatters golden and brown hair.

To discover which shades of GREEN suit YOU best, follow my draping method below. You will need:

- A mirror that is large enough to see yourself from the waist up.
- Lighting that is as bright and natural as possible. If you

must be in artificial light then use fluorescent bulbs.

- To stand against a background that is plain and colourless, preferably white.
- To remove all make-up (for women). You need a clean and clear face.
- To be clear of all jewellery round your neck.
- To keep your glasses on if you wear them so you can see yourself clearly.
- Some different shades of green to test against your face.
- To drape the shade of green over your shoulders making sure it reflects up against your skin.

What you WANT to see

1 An even skin tone
2 A reduction of skin blemishes and any high pink/red cheek colour
3 Your skin looking clear and fresh
4 Your eyes sparkling and the whites looking brighter
5 Your own natural colouring being enhanced
6 An absence of dark lines under the chin and shadows under the eyes
7 That the lines and wrinkles have lifted

What you DON'T want to see

8 An emphasis on skin blemishes
9 A patchy white complexion
10 Any red blotches
11 An accentuation of lines and wrinkles
12 An accentuation of dark shadows under the eyes or chin
13 A tired, unhealthy and dull appearance
14 A 'moustache' effect above your lip (which happens with very dark green)
15 Your lips looking darker (which happens with very dark green)

16   Roots in highlighted hair (which happens with very dark green)

Once you have done the above test, you should know which shades of green look fabulous on you and belong to your mindful colour palette and which ones you need to avoid. If you really can't tell, ask someone you can trust to be honest with you. The most important thing is that the shade should make you smile when you see yourself in it. If wearing green is not something that appeals to you then find a piece of jewellery with jade or emerald in it which will give you the same benefits, or choose an accessory item instead.

A case study – Louise

"When Jules asked me to appear on the *Chrissy B* Sky TV chat show with her, wearing my mindful colour of choice it simply had to be green! Having had my colours analysed with Jules as a spring, with a warm skin tone, golden brown hair and green eyes, I discovered that whilst I have lots of great shades to choose from in my individual colour palette, certain shades of green really make me feel great and are the ones I tend to get complimented in! When I went on the show I chose a particular green dress because I don't think there has been a time that I haven't been told how well I look and glowing when wearing it, so it really has become my WOW dress and as a result I have worn it to pieces. The girls on the show also loved it and I ended up being far more involved than I thought I would be, as they were keen to understand why this colour made me feel so much more confident. Simple really, this dress makes me feel young and happy."

Chapter 10

Mindfully *Blue – Choose your shade of blue and feel calm and in control*

Do you need to keep your nerves under control for optimum well-being?

Do you have a job interview and need to calmly communicate your skills and personality?

Are you starting a new venture and need to be cool and in control?

Are you giving a speech, or talking to people and need to be mindfully diplomatic?

Do you or your children need to feel composed when sitting exams?

Do you need to gain control over your weight or a physical problem?

Do you need some peace and quiet to recuperate during an illness or to ease anxiety?

Getting some blue into your life will help you emotionally, physically and psychologically. Before delving into the benefits of wearing blue and what shades will suit you best for optimum well-being, let's have a look at the background to this cool, comforting colour. It will help you to understand a bit about its power and why you may want to choose it as one of your mindful colours.

BLUE Background

It's official. Blue is the world's favourite colour! Whether it's because subconsciously so much of our world is blue, the sky and the sea, or whether it's because blue when viewed releases the hormone oxytocin, the relaxing, feel good hormone, that makes it so popular.

Blue's wavelength is shorter than red's, which is at the opposite end of the spectrum. It is restful and cool and the colour of trust, loyalty, diplomacy and clarity, and therefore used in many professions as a uniform, particularly in navy blue. For example the police, pilots, naval officers, and many in authority choose this colour.

In 2000 an experiment was undertaken in Glasgow, Scotland where blue street lighting was installed only in certain streets. These all reported fewer crimes than other neighbourhoods. This would seem to indicate that blue does indeed have a calming influence at a subconscious level.

Japan decided to experiment with blue lighting at 71 of their main train stations due to an increase in the number of suicides by persons diving in front of trains in the last few years. They installed blue light-emitting-diode (LED) lamps on the railway platforms and at railway crossings as a method of deterring suicides. The theory was that blue would help calm agitated and distressed commuters and would help to save lives as Japan's suicide rates have soared over recent years.

By using panel data between 2000 and 2010 from a railway company in a metropolitan area of Japan they looked at and compared the number of suicides before and after, and with and without the intervention of the blue lights. They used the number of suicides at 11 stations with the intervention as the treatment group and at the other 60 stations without the intervention as the control group.

Their analysis showed that the introduction of blue lights resulted in a staggering 84% decrease in the number of suicides, with the conclusion being that the blue lights are easier and less expensive to install than platform screen doors, so they can be used as a cost-effective method for suicide prevention. In Jodhpur in India the entire city is painted in differing shades of blue. Its inhabitants believe the colour keeps their homes cool in the blistering heat; it certainly looks beautiful.

Blue light is also now being used medically to treat skin conditions such as rosacea, which is very common and can cause facial flushing and redness. In America they are trialling a new drug called aminolevulinic acid that only works when activated by blue light, which means that beneficial effects can be targeted specifically to the areas that need treatment.

Blue is a calming, peaceful and pacifying colour; it also indicates depth and wisdom. It slows things down and lowers blood pressure, soothing the nervous system. It is an independent colour that allows for introversion and deep thinking.

The darker navy shades are businesslike to wear for work. The blue suit that is the mainstay of most business wardrobes for women and men first became fashionable as fitted attire in the 19th century in England. It was then adopted by London society and was originally a different coloured jacket and trousers, but by the late 19th century the single coloured suit had become fashionable albeit in black. It was then in the 20th century that blue and grey suits became popular. Nowadays the trouser suit is a big fashion statement. It says that women can compete in a man's world.

We all know the saying 'feeling blue' and because blue is a cool colour wearing too much of it in dark shades can become depressing. However, turquoise is a youthful, fun loving shade that uplifts the spirits, where very dark blue can sometimes dampen them.

Ask yourself what you need to do today and what emotions you are feeling that can be aided by mindfully wearing this universally loved colour. In this chapter you will learn all about how to get a sense of calm and control in a frazzled world.

The benefits of wearing BLUE

Do you need to keep your nerves under control for optimum well-being?

Blue is a wonderful colour to wear for calming your nervous

system as it releases the anti-stress and feel good hormone oxytocin. If you find yourself overloaded with stressful thoughts or too much to do, then wearing blue will help you to slow down the pace and create order out of chaos, creating peace of mind and the ability to be mindful in a calm and focussed way. If you have the need to withdraw mentally from any situation or a busy environment then wearing blue will help you to gain strength and inner centred-ness. Blue is the colour of tranquillity and peaceful communication helping you to stay cool in any situation.

For calmly communicating your skills in a mindful and diplomatic way

Blue should be one of your colours of choice for a job interview. This is because it is THE colour of communication, and with its ability to calm the nervous system it has the power to help you get across what you want to say which is crucial, and it will also help you to project your integrity. It also shows that you have faith in your own abilities and that you can be depended upon.

Blue is also seen as a corporate colour, so once you get a job wearing blue shows that you are good at communicating which is important in a new environment to demonstrate that you are open and honest. Blue is the colour of responsibility so people will quickly learn that they can rely on you. It also means that you have managerial aspirations and indicates a devotion to work and duty, structure and authority.

Blue represents someone who is good at planning and thinking, but make sure you consider combining blue with a colour that allows its calming effects to balance with the more dynamic elements of red, orange or yellow. It's great to have amazing thoughts but you also need a colour to enable you to action them. Wear a dark blue suit if you are interviewing for a job in the city or financial services, as a politician, lawyer, or teacher. Navy blue is authoritative and shows efficiency and detachment.

Blue is a colour to wear that shows others they can rely on you and that you are in control. Therefore it's perfect for certain environments, but in the media world or most caring professions navy blue could be seen as too severe. So wear blue to best effect as follows:

- The neck area is your powerhouse (throat chakra and energy centre) for communication so wear a blue scarf/tie or a smart piece of blue jewellery.
- Combine a navy blue jacket/suit with a coloured shirt of your choice and neutral (grey/black/beige/cream) trousers/skirt.
- Choose a blue shirt in a shade that suits you, with neutral coloured bottoms. Not too bright though, unless you are planning to work with children or in the media.
- Teaming a white shirt with a coloured jacket, navy blue trousers and shoes is smart.
- For a professional look, wear a blue dress for women or blue trousers for men, with a neutral coloured jacket (grey/navy/cream).
- If you don't choose to be seen in blue, wear it as underwear (in light or bright tones).
- Choose a blue handbag/briefcase and shoes in navy or cobalt, but not too bright.

For feeling composed in a stressful situation and when sitting exams

If you are going through a particularly stressful time, wear blue to calm you down. If you don't like blue as a colour then simply wear it at night as this will help with insomnia and ensure you get a good night's rest. If you can wear blue in some form during the day it will help in all areas of communication, be it with friends, partners or at work, and will also help to make others feel at ease with you. If you really have an aversion to wearing this colour then paint your bedroom blue or fill it with blue things you love!

If you or any of your loved ones are taking exams and have to wear a uniform wear some blue underwear as many people find exams a really stressful time and often panic, so choosing to wear blue will help enormously with nerves, enabling you to think more clearly and then you are able to quieten your mind.

For gaining control over your weight or a physical problem

Wearing blue physically calms you down if you find yourself overeating due to stress and anxiety. This in turn can help to stop this anxious period and re-evaluate why you are overeating. Also it would seem that blue foods are the least appetizing because they are often seen as having been spoilt and so not appealing to the human eye. There are certain plans available that suggest you eat off blue plates if you are trying to reduce your portions, as psychologically this will make you eat less.

As a soothing colour blue aids all inflammation, lowers blood pressure, and is also good for asthma and insomnia. However, if you are suffering from depression do NOT use this colour in its very dark shades or in large amounts because it can be too draining. Turquoise is fabulous to wear if your immune system is low as it will naturally boost it.

For getting some peace and quiet to recuperate during an illness or easing anxiety

Blue is a tonic for anyone craving some peace and quiet and when recovering from an illness, as it helps to calm and heal the body. Also if you are experiencing a period of anxiety or panic attacks particularly if going through an emotional trauma or a time of upheaval, when your body has gone out of balance, try wearing blue as this colour has the power to calm the nervous system.

When NOT to wear BLUE

Blue is not a good colour to wear in abundance if you are feeling lonely, withdrawn or depressed. If this is the case then particularly avoid dark shades of blue.

If BLUE is your No 1 mindful colour choice what does it say about your personality?

If your preference is for blue then you will display qualities of independence, and a quiet confidence and belief in yourself. You may find yourself in a position of leadership as your reliable and honest traits will allow others to trust you and enjoy your individuality.

Your calm nature in a crisis is admired and you crave support and equilibrium around you in order to thrive. With your caring and practical approach to life you make a reliable and dependable friend whom people often call upon for comfort and advice.

However, if you overindulge in the colour blue, you may tend to feel depressed or down in the dumps and end up in an isolated frame of mind. Also you may find yourself unable to let go of situations and people, becoming clingy. Make sure you balance your sense of value by combining other colours with blue – choose from my list below.

A special word on TURQUOISE

The ancient Persians revered turquoise as a stone because they believed it had such powerful protective abilities to keep them safe from evil. Many colour therapists feel that turquoise has different qualities to it, compared to the other blue shades.

I know that it is definitely the best blue for me, and I love the way it makes me feel. Turquoise is all about feelings of tranquillity, vitality, and freedom. It is an uplifting colour that can make you feel full of youthfulness and optimism. As turquoise is the combination of blue and green you can choose which shade appeals to you most by varying the proportions of each. Turquoise is **the** best colour to wear with a suntan as it highlights bronzed skin and it is the one universal colour that everyone can wear, whatever your skin tone and colouring. Just choose the shade that you like the best and the one that gets you the most compliments!

What colours to wear with BLUE?

- *ORANGE* is the complementary (opposite on the colour wheel) to blue and it will therefore automatically balance blue's cool, collective qualities by adding in some warmth and fun.
- *PEACH* is the softer version of orange and looks beautiful with paler blues.
- *YELLOW* and blue work wonderfully together for a blend of calm and joy. Wear a yellow top/shirt with denim jeans or navy trousers for getting your communicative skills across in a happy and optimistic manner.
- *PINK* looks wonderful with blue. Many women favour these combinations as pink shows off a loving, feminine nature and blue projects a dependable and trustworthy individual. Men are now getting into their feminine sides and often choose this colour to get in touch with their emotional needs.
- *RED* will fire up an individual with too much blue so it's a great combination to give some energy to blue's relaxed state.
- *WHITE* and *CREAM* look chic and smart with navy blue and also add freshness and clarity to all other blue shades, particularly in the warmer months.
- *BLACK* works well with the pale or brighter shades of blue. Dark blue and black are only advisable for very cool

colouring and they can be draining on the skin and energy, so wear with care. It will also give an impression of seriousness so only appropriate in a work environment.

Different shades of BLUE and which ones suit YOU best

Once you have decided you feel like wearing blue, which shade do you choose for optimum well-being? It is pointless to wear a blue jacket because you feel emotionally in need of this colour only to discover the shade washes you out and makes you look tired and unhealthy. Obviously this is counterproductive to you looking and feeling your best.

There are many words to describe the different varieties of blue: periwinkle, sky, cobalt, electric, cornflower, air force, royal, denim, Persian, to name just a few, but which one will make you look radiant and healthy, with a glowing complexion and sparkling eyes? Your colouring will determine which shades of blue suit you best. To keep things simple there are 4 categories that blue falls into: either pale pastel blue or pure blue for cool skin tones, royal blue or blue-green for warm skin tones.

1   Pale pastel blue is very flattering for pink based cool summer skins and particularly gorgeous if you also have blue eyes.

2   Pure cool electric and cobalt blue can be really stunning on a blue-eyed very cool and dramatic winter skin tone. Navy blue is also very harmonious with this colouring.

3   Royal bright blue for yellow/golden spring skins is glorious as is bright turquoise. If you also have blue or green eyes you have many bright warm shades to choose from.

4   Blue-green or teal is best if you have a bronze based autumn complexion. If you have brown eyes and hair then these are your best shades of blue.

To discover which shades of BLUE suit YOU best, follow my draping method below. You will need:

- A mirror that is large enough to see yourself from the waist up.
- Lighting that is as bright and natural as possible. If you must be in artificial light then use fluorescent bulbs.
- To stand against a background that is plain and colourless, preferably white.
- For women to remove all make-up. You need a clean and clear face.
- Be clear of all jewellery round your neck.
- To keep your glasses on if you wear them so you can see yourself clearly.
- Some different shades of blue to test against your face.
- To drape the blue shade over your shoulders making sure it reflects against your skin.

What you WANT to see

1   An even skin tone
2   A reduction in skin blemishes
3   Your skin looking clearer and fresher
4   Your eyes sparkling and the whites looking brighter
5   Your own natural colouring enhanced
6   An absence of dark lines under the chin and shadows under the eyes
7   That your lines and wrinkles have been lifted

What you DON'T want to see

8   An emphasis on skin blemishes
9   A patchy white, washed-out complexion
10   Any red blotches
11   An accentuation of lines and wrinkles
12   An accentuation of dark shadows under the eyes or chin
13   A tired, unhealthy appearance

14 A 'moustache' effect above your lip (which can happen with very dark blue)

15 Your lips looking darker (which can happen with very dark blue)

16 Roots in highlighted hair (which can happen with very dark blue)

Please note that navy blue can have the same detrimental and ageing effects as black because often this shade has black behind it. Many people think as they age that switching from black to navy blue is doing them big favours, when actually dark navy will do the same damage. If you have a choice, keep to air force or royal blue, and if you do choose to wear navy keep it away from your face. That way it won't highlight any dark areas, lines or shadows that you want to avoid making more visible!

Once you have done the above test, you should know which shades of blue look fabulous on you and belong to your mindful colour palette, and which ones you need to avoid. If you really can't tell, then ask someone you can trust to be honest with you. The most important thing is that the shade should make you smile when you see yourself in it. If wearing blue doesn't appeal to you then consider a blue stone in some jewellery like sapphire or lapis lazuli, as it will give you the same benefits. Alternatively buy some blue accessories like scarves, ties, belts, shoes or bags or wear hidden as underwear.

A case study – Liz

Liz is an outstanding woman, who not only runs her own successful clothing business but who also looks after a large family, which includes a husband, four children, one grandchild and her mother-in-law. Liz relies on blue to keep her focussed and in control when working and looking after so many people.

When I first met her many years ago she used to wear very pale, washed-out pastel shades of pinks, blues and a lot of white.

With light blonde hair, blue eyes and a golden, warm based skin tone which tans beautifully, these colours were making her look incredibly pale – something she disliked but didn't realise until she started to wear brighter colours.

Liz says wearing blue calms her down in a fairly hectic home environment where she finds herself juggling many jobs. "It's become the staple colour in my wardrobe and one that I always reach for if I have a particularly stressful day as it helps me to cope emotionally and keeps me looking my best.

I have always loved blue but was clearly wearing the wrong shades because seeing how much younger and healthier I looked in bright blues, cobalt and turquoise was a revelation. So I started wearing them all the time, and at work so many women complimented me and asked me if they could buy the same dresses that I began selling them."

Chapter 11

Mindfully *Purple – Choose your shade of purple and feel inspired and creative*

Do you have a broken heart that needs healing?

Are you going through difficult times of change?

Do you need strength and stability after suffering from grief or distress?

Are you craving some self-respect and strength due to a major life change: a house move or retirement?

Do you need help recuperating after a long illness?

Is it necessary for you to be the peacemaker in a difficult relationship?

Getting some purple into your life will help you emotionally, physically and psychologically. Before delving into the benefits of wearing purple and what shades will suit you best for optimum well-being, let's have a look at the background to this wonderfully healing and transformational colour. It will help you to understand a bit about its power and why you may want to choose it as one of your mindful colours.

PURPLE Background

Purple is a mixture of red and blue and is a non-spectral colour. Its counterpart violet is a spectral colour and has the shortest wavelength being the final colour of the seven rays of the full rainbow spectrum of light. Whilst violet is not seen as such an intense colour as purple they share similar psychological meanings as they both contain the strength of red and the calming values of blue.

Purple is the colour of purpose and dedication. Wearing it will increase feelings of self-worth and dignity, and take you into the realms of spiritual awareness and a depth of feeling you might not have yet experienced. It connects you to your higher consciousness, and can help you feel mentally at peace.

Wearing purple will help you to get in touch with the unconditionally loving side of your nature. We all have the ability to feel love at this deep level but sometimes find it hard to get in touch with it – purple encourages compassion at all levels.

As a colour, purple strives to stand out from the crowd and be individual and different. If you are creative you will love to wear this colour and hopefully will find it inspiring as it combines wisdom and the sensitivity to help others. Purple is a powerful colour and will help you to get in touch with your leadership qualities. It is the most calming and healing of all the colours and encompasses shades from indigo, to violet and magenta.

Purple is also the colour of transformation, and wearing it can help you take on your spiritual lessons and learn from them. It suggests power, mystery and sophistication.

In Medieval times purple dye was very expensive to produce and today we associate the colour with royalty, and also the high church, representing spiritual wisdom and authority. In our modern world it has become a popular colour to wear for world leaders. It is particularly favoured by men choosing their tie colours, being more active than blue and less aggressive than red.

Dating back to the Old Testament when the shade "Tyrian purple" was mentioned as a coloured cloth, this became the chosen colour for great leaders like Alexander the Great. The Romans wore purple togas as did the magistrates and priests. It was a colour indulged in Renaissance paintings, often used when depicting angels or the Virgin Mary.

In China purple symbolises spiritualism, in Japan it is the colour of privilege and wealth, and in Thailand it is their colour of mourning. In the 20th century, it took up modern day royal connections when firstly donned by George VI and later Queen Elizabeth II who decided to use it as a primary colour in her coronation. Purple also became one of the three colours that symbolised the Suffragette movement which finally succeeded in gaining the vote for women. In the 1970s purple became the colour synonymous with psychedelic drugs and with musicians like Jimi Hendrix and Deep Purple.

Purple as a colour occurs the least in nature. Plants and foods have this colour because they contain a pigment called anthocyanin. This helps to promote photosynthesis in plants and aids in the attraction of insects to pollenate flowers.

Purple and its shades relate to your higher mind and stimulate the imagination. It is able to help with mental conditions, bringing calm into a troubled mind, and when combined with pink can ease a broken heart. Purple (and violet) are generally introverted colours and wearing them can indicate your desire to be left alone for a period of deep thought and reflection.

As a healing colour, purple purifies the blood, bringing calm to your body. It is a great colour to use for any health issues relating to your head, ears, migraines, sinuses and scalp problems.

The benefits of wearing PURPLE

Do you have a broken heart that needs healing?

Have you recently had your heart broken? Perhaps you are coming out of a destructive relationship that has left you seeking a new purpose in your life? If you are ready to face these deep emotional issues then purple really can help you to find peace and move on.

Wearing purple and violet in particular will make you feel unshakable. Violet also has the ability to calm a chaotic mind, to help you learn lessons from your past experiences, and then allow new changes to come into your life. Wearing purple with pink is a particularly powerful combination in times of emotional healing and to ease a broken heart.

Are you going through difficult times of change?

Embracing change can be daunting and difficult. If you are struggling with relationship dilemmas then wearing purple will help you to embrace change and can offer emotional protection. Purple is a balancing colour, restoring equilibrium into any situations that might throw you off course.

The tendency to take on too much and become stressed can result in headaches and eye strain. Shades of purple will help to bring the mind into focus, and allow clear thinking and creativity to flow. Wearing this colour will also project a conscientious image.

Do you need strength and stability after suffering grief or distress?

If you have been suffering a period of emotional or physical distress or grief, then wearing purple can be wonderfully healing and uplifting. It can instil feelings of stability and strength at a time when you can feel out of control or unable to find any light at the end of a dark tunnel. Purple is a colour that can connect you to your deepest intuitive nature. Your mind will find some calm and peace, and it may help you to seek meditation or other forms of relaxation to help you through a difficult grieving or distressed time. If you need to take some time out for quiet contemplation then wear violet in particular. It will also help you to gain a vision of a positive future based on goals and inspiration. Wearing this colour will help you to focus on happiness through change and embrace positive opportunities.

Are you craving self-respect due to a major life change, a house move or retirement?

After experiencing a major life change, it can be hard to find focus and inner calm when all you feel is upheaval. If your children are leaving home this can be experienced as a time of liberation, but for others it can be a lonely and emotionally devastating period of adjustment. If you have stayed at home to bring up your family then it can be much harder, because it feels like the job you have dedicated yourself to for many years has suddenly made you redundant.

Redundancy from the workforce can be just as hard to bear. You may have spent many years working in companies that have given you an everyday purpose. Being with people and having a value that is paid for, it can seem incredibly daunting when suddenly left at home with no job to go to.

Also if you have recently moved house you will be adjusting to new locations, neighbours and energies. These are all demanding and life-changing, stressful situations.

Wearing purple will help you to connect with yourself and get in touch with your spirituality so that you can understand your higher purpose in life at a time when you may be questioning how to plan and live your future. Purple can give you a renewed sense of purpose and an independence you now find yourself able to indulge in.

Do you need help recuperating after an illness?

Purple is a colour that relates particularly to the head and any problems to the upper part of the body. It corresponds to the main pituitary gland which lies at the base of the brain and regulates your hormones, but it is also connected to mental health issues too. In particular it is a colour recommended for any problems with your eyes, ears, nose and scalp.

If you have been suffering a period of illness then you may feel exhausted on a physical as well as a mental level. Wearing purple will give you a sense of healing by promoting strength and stability, emitting a calming and peaceful ray throughout your body. Often when you are unwell you want to be left alone to deal with your aches and pains. This colour will provide you with an invisible barrier from others' demands and emotions so that you have time to heal emotionally and physically, to retreat before recovery.

Is it necessary for you to be the peacemaker in a difficult relationship?

When Christmas approaches I am often asked which colour would be best to help people cope through such a stressful and demanding period. Not only are there endless lists of things to buy and food to prepare, but it is often a time when relations all come together to celebrate but which can sometimes end in conflict. Not everyone gets on. There are often tensions and heated debates and disagreements with loved ones particularly over decisions that have to be made.

So purple is one of the best colours to wear for peacemaking at Christmas and any time of the year when experiencing problems in relationships. It will give you a sense of purpose and focus in a calm and peaceful way to still troubled waters in difficult relationships using sensitivity and compassion. Wearing purple or violet will give you the clarity and depth of intuition to make a real difference to problem solving.

When NOT to wear PURPLE

If you are feeling depressed, then please keep clear of wearing this colour. Also if you tend to daydream too much and fantasise, don't wear it!

If PURPLE is your No 1 mindful colour choice what does it say about your personality?

Wearing purple as your mindfully chosen colour means that you are compassionate and caring, with a sensitive side. You love helping others and are motivated by giving. You have a lovely peaceful quality that draws people to you and they often offload their problems on to you too. You are probably introverted by nature, but not to be mistaken for shy. You will have a charisma that is very appealing and a visionary mind, and keep away from following a crowd. With your natural free-spirited personality you have a desire to travel and experience new cultures. Beware wearing too much purple as it can make you moody, so try and balance it with some magenta to bring out your naturally intuitive and charismatic personality. Also wear yellow or gold with purple in order to allow your fun loving side to come through.

What colours to wear with PURPLE?

There are certain colours that work beautifully with purple. Some enhance its royal essence, whilst others balance its introversion:

- *YELLOW* is the complementary colour (opposite on the colour wheel) to purple. When worn together yellow brings a well needed balance to purple's tendency for introversion as it brings out a cheerful nature and the ability to have fun.

- *ORANGE* and purple worn together are not for the faint-hearted! Particularly when I see women wearing these colours in their strongest shades it is a visually dynamic and stunning combination. So you need to feel confident about carrying them off in anything other than small amounts. Orange will add sociability to purple's calm and peaceful qualities so this pairing makes a powerful duo.

- *PINK* and purple together bring out the best of each other, and for women are pretty and feminine. If you need to nurture and protect yourself and find your inner strength then wear these two loving colours together.

- *WHITE* and *CREAM* blend well with the lavender shades which look pretty in the warmer months and are a good combination to wear at work. These neutral tones will give purple's visionary appeal a professional edge.

- *BLACK* and purple are very striking and look vibrant in the cooler months. Creative people love this combination as purple and violet will encourage all areas of positive change which works well with black's ability to control situations.

Different shades of PURPLE and which ones suit YOU best

Once you have decided you feel like wearing purple, which shade do you choose for ultimate well-being? The right purple on the right person can stop traffic! However, beware of the wrong shade because purple is one of those colours that can make you look washed out. Your individual colouring will determine which shade of purple suits you best. As with any new colour you haven't worn before please purchase an inexpensive top or tie to start with in order to see how you feel about wearing it and what comments you get. If it's a success then you can gradually add more of this colour to your wardrobe.

To keep things simple there are 4 categories that purple falls into: cool light lavender, cool deep purple, warm blue-violet and warm pure violet.

1 Cool light lavender and mauve are very flattering on soft, delicate summer colouring.
2 Cool deep purple or red-purple look striking on strong cool winter colouring with distinct features, particularly with black or very dark hair.
3 Warm blue-violet can look fabulous on spring redheads and warm skinned blondes.
4 Warm pure violet is strong and dynamic on autumn's dark bronze based complexions and brunettes with red undertones.

To discover which shades of PURPLE suit you best, follow my draping method below. You will need:

- A mirror that is large enough to see yourself from the waist up.
- Lighting that is as bright and natural as possible. If you must be in artificial light then use fluorescent bulbs.
- To stand against a background that is plain and colourless, preferably white.
- For women to remove all make-up. You need a clean and clear face.
- Be clear of all jewellery round your neck.
- To keep your glasses on if you wear them so you can see yourself clearly.
- Some different shades of purple to test against your face.
- To drape purple over your shoulders making sure it reflects up against your skin.

What you WANT to see

1   An even skin tone
2   A reduction of skin blemishes
3   Your skin looking clear and fresh
4   Your eyes sparkling and the whites looking brighter
5   Your own natural colouring enhanced
6   An absence of dark lines under the chin and shadows under the eyes
7   That the lines and wrinkles have lifted

What you DON'T want to see

8   An emphasis on skin blemishes
9   A patchy white and washed-out complexion
10   Any red blotches
11   An accentuation of lines and wrinkles
12   An accentuation of dark shadows under the eyes or chin
13   A tired, unhealthy appearance

14 A 'moustache' effect above your lip (which can happen with very dark purple)

15 Your lips looking darker (which can happen with very dark purple)

16 Roots in highlighted hair (which can happen with very dark purple)

Once you have done the above test, you should know which shades of purple look fabulous on you and belong to your mindful colour palette, and which ones you need to avoid. If you really can't tell, ask someone you can trust to be honest with you. The most important thing is that the shade should make you smile when you see yourself in it.

If you just don't find a shade you like and that suits you, wear some purple coloured jewellery like amethyst which will provide you with the wonderfully calming and protective powers of purple's wavelength.

Also consider purple accessories such as scarves, ties, handbags and shoes. Wearing purple underwear against your skin will allow the qualities of this transformational colour to be absorbed into your system.

A case study – Nina

Nina is an incredibly brave and inspirational lady. She was diagnosed with terminal cancer in 2012 and has written a book called *The Adventures of a Cancer Maverick*. This is how purple makes her feel.

"I adore the colour purple for many reasons. The first, and probably most important reason, is that it was my mum's favourite colour. I remember in the 70s we had a very avant-garde glossy kitchen, and the units were a deep delicious aubergine colour.

She loved to wear any shade of purple too. In fact, she wore lilac to my wedding and has never looked more glamorous. My mum passed away in November 2011, and we all wore something purple at her funeral. She would've found that very pleasing on the eye.

It has now become a bit of a shorthand way of feeling connected to her – wearing purple makes me feel secure, and it makes me smile remembering the amazing times we had, and her unconditional love for me. Wow. How powerful is that!

I had a big Purple moment in late 2012. I was out doing a bit of retail therapy with my sister, when I found the most beautiful winter coat. It was that gorgeous deep Cadbury purple. It looked like it had come straight from a 50s movie – fitted waist, flared skirt. I loved it. I remember looking at the coat with a tear in my eye. You see I had just been diagnosed with terminal cancer – not really the time to be making such an investment purchase. I didn't know that I would be able to wear it through that winter, never mind any subsequent ones.

My sister gently told me that I shouldn't think like that and whisked off to buy it for me. It felt like a real vote of confidence in me, that I would still be around to enjoy it.

Whenever I wear it, I feel a million dollars, and maybe it's no coincidence that I have worn the coat a lot, and we are now in 2014. That's my kind of medicine!"

Chapter 12

Mindfully Neutral – *Choose your shades of GREY, BLACK, BROWN or WHITE and feel complete*

What neutral colour can make you feel independent and competent? Would you like to show leadership qualities whilst looking smart and chic?
What colour is both a traditional and practical wardrobe addition? What neutral colours will balance any outfit whilst portraying optimism and clarity?

Coordinate your wardrobe with neutral shades

Neutrals are colours that should be able to remain in your wardrobe for many years, forming the basis of your colour schemes. Whilst other colours come and go in the fashion stakes, your neutrals should always be present, so spending a bit more on classic items like coats, jackets and cardigans is something to consider. This is when sale shopping can be at its most constructive.

Neutrals have a very important role to play in most wardrobes, as they balance outfits and can 'tone down' anything bright or bold. If you are having a 'neutral' day when you either don't feel like wearing any colour, or it is a requirement for your work, then make sure you mindfully choose the ones that suit you best. People tend to enjoy wearing neutrals because they are considered 'safe': they go with everything, don't stand out or make bold statements.

Knowing whether you have the cool colouring that looks good in a grey suit or a beige one will make a lot of difference to getting your neutrals to combine with the rest of your wardrobe. Neutral colours such as beige, grey, black, white or cream whilst appearing to be colourless can actually have underlying warm or cool tones.

So, let's take a look at the neutral shades, and see which ones you feel are most appropriately suited to your colouring, and combine best with your mindful colour palette and your lifestyle.

How GREY can make you feel independent and competent

Choosing to wear grey as one of your neutral colours can have great benefits. Firstly it portrays someone who is detached, independent and professional. It shows you handle stress in a balanced way with fair judgement, so this is one of the best colours to wear in a working environment. It was also voted by industries as one of the top business colours. If you want to be seen as someone who is solid and reliable and can behave in a self-controlled and practical manner, choose grey.

Grey is a combination of black and white and predominantly cool so wonderful for all of you with the summer or winter colouring. Grey with blue added to it will also flatter your complexion. If, however, you have a warm spring or autumn skin tone, a grey that has a hint of yellow or red behind it will look lovely and generally be kinder to your face than wearing black.

Grey looks fabulous when worn with most colours; simply tailor how pale or dark, warm or cool your chosen shades are depending on your own individual colouring. I don't recommend wearing ALL grey as this can indicate a lack of personality, so always try and add some colour into a grey outfit, however small. It will benefit your mood as well as how others view you.

How BLACK conveys leadership and is smart and chic

Black is the darkest colour and the absence of light. A shade of black is simply a colour mixed with black otherwise known as off-black, i.e. ebony, charcoal, onyx, jet, liquorice and black olive.

As a neutral colour black provides a dramatic contrast to other colours, giving them a formality and a distinction.

Let's be honest, most women LOVE black! It is viewed as the best colour to wear to hide lumps and bumps, a smart and chic way to coordinate wardrobes, easy to grab first thing in the morning, versatile with colours, and everyone needs a Little Black Dress – right?

Right for those cool skinned winter women out there but not so good for warmer skinned ones, and that goes for men who love black too! Black works brilliantly in so many situations and is of course a staple for most wardrobes. However, please ensure having done the draping test in this book that you are one of those people who can wear it well up against your face without it showing any of the detrimental signs of ageing and draining, and this applies to men as well as women. If you are someone who looks better with it away from your face then please do continue to wear it in abundance if you love it. However, make sure you wear your mindfully chosen best colours close to your complexion to make sure you get complimented every day, and for ultimate well-being.

So what qualities does black have to offer your life and wardrobe? Black gives the impression that you are in control and it conveys leadership. In a working environment it is best kept for managerial positions as it is a very authoritative colour and can therefore be seen as overpowering, in positions of assistants for instance.

If wearing black trousers or skirts, try and wear a different coloured blazer, jacket or shirt/blouse. For men, black suits can be brightened up with coloured ties. Also consider keeping black to your accessories only, i.e. bags/briefcases, shoes and belts.

How BROWN is a traditional and practical wardrobe addition

Brown isn't strictly a neutral colour, but a composite one, i.e. it is made by mixing other colours together and not the absence of colour. You can achieve different shades of brown by mixing orange and black; red, yellow and black; red and green. Brown can be light or dark, warm; reddish or yellowish or cool; grey-brown.

Brown is conservative and traditional. It portrays someone who is practical, down to earth and reliable and who values stability and structure. The warmer shades of brown such as caramel, chestnut, rich auburn, coffee can be worn in abundance by autumn individuals in their colour palette up against their complexions as it brings out their golden/bronzed underlying skin tones and harmonises with them. So in this case, brown can be worn as a neutral colour instead of black.

If you have the spring colouring then brown is best worn in the warm shades of camel or tan. If you are a cool summer with a soft, pale complexion the light taupe shades are best. With a winter cool complexion then you can wear dark chocolate brown as well as black.

Brown works beautifully in combination with orange, turquoise, reds and bright green. Beware of wearing too much brown in one outfit; always try and include one of your favourite mindful colours.

How WHITE and CREAM will balance any outfit with optimism

White and cream can either have a warm or a cool undertone. Warm hints could be yellow, peach or beige, whilst cool hints grey, pink or blue. Make sure you stick to the ones that suit your own individual skin tone. My draping test will have helped you to discover whether white or cream suits you best.

Mixing white or cream with your wardrobe colours will give the impression that you are well balanced and optimistic, that you are orderly and enjoy clarity of thought. Being naturally receptive you have a direct approach to life and need to be respected for your opinions.

White or cream are seen as professional in working environments, and in most situations will add freshness to any outfit when combined with your mindful colours that make you look and feel your best.

Chapter 13

Mindfully Choose Your Own Colourful Conclusion

My aim in this book has been to help people of any age, nationality or background to take control of their colours, to consciously choose which ones can help physically, emotionally and psychologically in all aspects of life, because everyone deserves to look great, and feel happy and balanced.

So, I hope this book has encouraged you to feel excited about experimenting with and embracing new colours into your wardrobe. Choosing to take control of how you dress every day can be truly empowering, save you time and energy not to mention money too!

I have been privileged to work with people from many walks of life from celebrities, TV presenters, teachers, business executives, housewives, and sixth form students, helping to educate them on how the colours they choose to wear can positively enhance their lives.

I often get asked who my role model is and for many years it has been the Queen, because she wears colours in such a mindful way: the ones that harmonise with her personal colouring, complement her personality and project the perfect image for her position. I was lucky enough to appear on breakfast television a few years ago talking about colours for the Queen's Jubilee and I felt thrilled to be able to highlight just how inspirational she is with her colour and style choices, for all the nation to benefit. Her favourite colour appears to be blue, and what better choice to project an image of diplomacy, tact and dependability, to support her communication skills, whilst keeping her calm and controlled in such a highly visible and influential role.

So the next time you see the Queen in the media, notice how

beautifully colour coordinated she is and take inspiration from our 'Queen of colour-block', and rest assured you don't have to be royalty to look as splendid as she does!

I wish you all a colourful life.

Acknowledgements

I must mindfully mention everyone who not only contributed to the content of this book, but those who supported me throughout its process. Lou, Fee, Jen, Georgie, Charlotte, Susie, Janie, Lizzie and Rachel for being such amazing friends, along with Andrew, Iain, Philip, Mark, Tilly, Helen, Carina, Kuldeep, Wendy, Ann, Nina, Millie, Victoria, Andrea and Ase, all whose input was invaluable.

To my mum who luckily for me continues to be a huge inspiration in my life, my supportive bookend Justin, my wonderful rock Miles, and Becca and Alex who will always be my greatest achievements!

Thanks to all at John Hunt Publishing for commissioning this book, my second with them, and to everyone involved in the process from believing in its initial concept to getting it into the marketplace, and all the hard work that goes on in between.

Thank you also to Pat and Ray at Colourflair whose belief and support in me has been continuous, and their wonderful colour knowledge has of course been the basis of all my consultations, teachings and writing to date.

And finally a big thank you to all the staff at Ansell & Clarke, particularly Alex who puts up with my lack of computer savvy, and who work tirelessly behind the scenes on my website.

Book References

The Author

Jules Standish is "The Colour Counsellor", a Colour and Style expert and tutor
For personal consultations, presentations on colour, corporate events, training:
email jules@colourconsultancy.co.uk
www.colourconsultancy.co.uk

References and Quotations

Chrissy B – Producer and Presenter
www.chrissybshow.tv

Wendy Elsmore – Fashion and Style Expert, the London College of Style
www.londoncollegeofstyle.com
+44(020) 3096 9966

Kuldeep Channa – TV Producer/Director
http://uk.linkedin.com/pub/kuldeep-channa/13/635/70
Reiki Practitioner – www.kcreikiandhealing.weebly.com

Helen Kendall-Tobias – Personal Image and Health Consultant, training with Imagination and Colourflair
www.imaginationonline.info
www.colourflair.co.uk

Nina Joy – Inspirational Speaker, Maverick Mentor and Author of *The Adventures of a Cancer Maverick* and *How to be a Cancer Maverick*
www.ninajoy.com

Dr Marilyn Glenville – PhD, Nutritionist, Public Speaker and Author of numerous books including *New Natural Alternatives to HRT*
www.marilynglenville.com
www.naturalhealthpractice.com

Carina Bayley – Body Control Pilates Master Mat and Equipment Instructor/Studio Owner
Posture Perfect Pilates
www.cbayley.com

Lizzie Velasquez – Public Speaker and Author
http://www.aboutlizzie.com

Mia Törnblom – Motivational Speaker/Leadership Coach and Author of *Self-Esteem Now!*
www.mtgruppen.com

Ase Greenacre – Personal Performance and Parent Coach
www.greatdevelopment.co.uk
07720 591857

Action Medical Research UK
action.org.uk/events

Andrew Jose – Leading London Hairstylist
Andrew@andrewjose.com

Alison Lurie – Author, *The Language of Clothes*

Thelma van der Werff – Author, *Let Colour Be Thy Medicine*

Susan Bixler and Nancy Nix-Rice – Co-authors, *The New Professional Image*

Elisabeth Kübler-Ross – Psychiatrist and Author (co-author David Kessler), *On Grief and Grieving: Finding the Meaning of Grief Through the Five Stages of Loss*

Jo Paoletti – Author, *Pink and Blue: Telling the Boys from the Girls in America*

Psychologies Magazine
www.psychologies.co.uk

Tilly Maclay – Photographer

Russell Foster – Professor of Circadian Neuroscience at Oxford University

Amanda Platell – Journalist

Mariella Frostrup – TV Presenter

Eileen Durward – Health Expert

Daniela Spath – Psychologist

Valerie Morris – Naomi Campbell's mother
Kim Freshwater – Slimmer of year 2013 quotation
Christian Dior – Fashion Designer
Coco Chanel – Fashion Designer
Frank Sinatra – Singer, actor
Audrey Hepburn – Actress
L'Oréal – Hair products
"Yahoo Shine", Midge Wilson, PhD – Professor of psychology at DePaul University
Superdrug – Chemist
Robert Burton – Researcher quoted in the *Telegraph*
Johann Wolfgang Goethe – Philosopher
Max Lüscher – Swiss professor of psychology
Faber Birren – American art historian

Other Books by Jules Standish

How Not to Wear Black
Published by O-Books (www.o-books.net)
ISBN 978-1-84694-561-8
Available to purchase on www.amazon.co.uk and
www.amazon.com and all major bookstores

BOOKS

O-BOOKS

SPIRITUALITY

O is a symbol of the world, of oneness and unity; this eye represents knowledge and insight. We publish titles on general spirituality and living a spiritual life. We aim to inform and help you on your own journey in this life. If you have enjoyed this book, why not tell other readers by posting a review on your preferred book site? Recent bestsellers from O-Books are:

The Heart of Tantric Sex
Diana Richardson
Revealing Eastern secrets of deep love and intimacy to Western couples.
Paperback: 978-1-90381-637-0 e-book: 978-1-84694-637-0

Crystal Prescriptions
The A-Z guide to over 1,200 symptoms and their healing crystals
Judy Hall
The first in the popular series of four books, this handy little guide is packed as tight as a pill-bottle with crystal remedies for ailments.
Paperback: 978-1-90504-740-6 e-book: 978-1-84694-629-5

Take Me To Truth
Undoing the Ego
Nouk Sanchez, Tomas Vieira
The best-selling step-by-step book on shedding the Ego, using
the teachings of *A Course In Miracles*.
Paperback: 978-1-84694-050-7 e-book: 978-1-84694-654-7

7 Myths about Love...Actually!
The journey from your HEAD to the HEART of your SOUL
Mike George
Smashes all the myths about LOVE.
Paperback: 978-1-84694-288-4 e-book: 978-1-84694-682-0

The Holy Spirit's Interpretation of the New Testament
A course in Understanding and Acceptance
Regina Dawn Akers
Following on from the strength of *A Course in Miracles*, NTI
teaches us how to experience the love and oneness of God.
Paperback: 978-1-84694-085-9 e-book: 978-1-78099-083-5

The Message of A Course In Miracles
A translation of the text in plain language
Elizabeth A. Cronkhite
A translation of *A Course in Miracles* into plain, everyday
language for anyone seeking inner peace. The companion
volume, *Practicing a Course In Miracles*, offers practical lessons
and mentoring.
Paperback: 978-1-84694-319-5 e-book: 978-1-84694-642-4

Rising in Love

My Wild and Crazy Ride to Here and Now, with Amma, the
Hugging Saint

Ram Das Batchelder

Rising in Love conveys an author's extraordinary journey of
spiritual awakening with the Guru, Amma.

Paperback: 978-1-78279-687-9 e-book: 978-1-78279-686-2

The Thinker's Guide to God

Peter Vardy

An introduction to key issues in the philosophy of religion.

Paperback: 978-1-90381-622-6

Your Simple Path

Find happiness in every step

Ian Tucker

A guide to helping us reconnect with what is really important in
our lives.

Paperback: 978-1-78279-349-6 e-book: 978-1-78279-348-9

365 Days of Wisdom

Daily Messages To Inspire You Through The Year

Dadi Janki

Daily messages which cool the mind, warm the heart and guide
you along your journey.

Paperback: 978-1-84694-863-3 ebook: 978-1-84694-864-0

Body of Wisdom

Women's Spiritual Power and How it Serves

Hilary Hart

Bringing together the dreams and experiences of women across
the world with today's most visionary spiritual teachers.

Paperback: 978-1-78099-696-7 ebook: 978-1-78099-695-0

Dying to Be Free
From Enforced Secrecy to Near Death to True Transformation
Hannah Robinson
After an unexpected accident and near-death experience,
Hannah Robinson found herself radically transforming her life,
while a remarkable new insight altered her relationship with
her father; a practising Catholic priest.
Paperback: 978-1-78535-254-6 ebook: 978-1-78535-255-3

The Ecology of the Soul
A Manual of Peace, Power and Personal Growth for Real People
in the Real World
Aidan Walker
Balance your own inner Ecology of the Soul to regain your
natural state of peace, power and wellbeing.
Paperback: 978-1-78279-850-7 ebook: 978-1-78279-849-1

Not I, Not other than I
The Life and Teachings of Russel Williams
Steve Taylor, Russel Williams
The miraculous life and inspiring teachings of one of the
World's greatest living Sages.
Paperback: 978-1-78279-729-6 ebook: 978-1-78279-728-9

On the Other Side of Love
A woman's Unconventional Journey Towards Wisdom
Muriel Maufroy
When life has lost all meaning, what do you do?
Paperback: 978-1-78535-281-2 ebook: 978-1-78535-282-9

Practicing A Course In Miracles

A Translation of the Workbook in Plain Language and With
Mentoring Notes
Elizabeth A. Cronkhite
The practical second and third volumes of *The Plain-Language A
Course in Miracles*.
Paperback: 978-1-84694-403-1 ebook: 978-1-78099-072-9

Quantum Bliss

The Quantum Mechanics of Happiness, Abundance, and Health
George S. Mentz
Quantum Bliss is the breakthrough summary of success and
spirituality secrets that customers have been waiting for.
Paperback: 978-1-78535-203-4 ebook: 978-1-78535-204-1

The Upside Down Mountain

Mags MacKean
A must-read for anyone weary of chasing success and happiness
– one woman's inspirational journey swapping the uphill slog
for the downhill slope.
Paperback: 978-1-78535-171-6 ebook: 978-1-78535-172-3

Your Personal Tuning Fork

The Endocrine System
Deborah Bates
Discover your body's health secret, the endocrine system, and
'twang' your way to sustainable health!
Paperback: 978-1-84694-503-8 ebook: 978-1-78099-697-4